Food for Today

Vegetables

Food for Today

Food for Today

Vegetables

Margaret Cullen

Illustrated by
Maurice Hutchings

Heinemann Educational Books
London

LONDON   EDINBURGH   MELBOURNE
AUCKLAND   TORONTO   HONG KONG
SINGAPORE   KUALA LUMPUR   NEW DELHI
NAIROBI   JOHANNESBURG   LUSAKA
IBADAN   KINGSTON

ISBN 0 435 42465 3

Published by Heinemann Educational Books Ltd
48 Charles Street, London W1X 8AH
Printed in Great Britain by
Biddles Ltd, Guildford, Surrey

Contents

Part 1

Introductory Note

All the recipes are in metric measurement. If you have to use scales showing only imperial measurements translate the kilos and grams into pounds and ounces before you start. Take 25 g to equal 1 oz as the base unit.

In every case the 'spoon' measurements refer to level spoonfuls. Where possible use British standard measuring spoons for capacity measurements rather than ordinary spoons. If these are not available use the equivalents listed below:

15 ml	1 tablespoon
10 ml	1 dessertspoon
5 ml	1 teaspoon
2.5 ml	½ teaspoon
1.25 ml	¼ teaspoon

Unless otherwise stated, the vegetables to be used in the recipes are fresh raw vegetables.

If you are using frozen or canned vegetables remember that frozen vegetables take a shorter time than fresh vegetables to cook and that canned vegetables are already cooked. Adapt the preparation instructions and the cooking time of the recipes to allow for this.

Dried vegetables should be soaked in water according to the instructions on the pack before using them for these recipes.

If you use stock cubes to make stock, bear in mind that these are often heavily salted so season with care having tasted the food first.

The recipe section of this book is arranged in alphabetical order under each vegetable. Further information about the vegetables will be found in the Vegetables A to Z section which starts on page 65. This section is also arranged alphabetically.

Vegetable Recipes

ARTICHOKES (GLOBE)

Globe artichokes discolour easily. Avoid using carbon steel knives or cooking them in aluminium saucepans.

Boiled Whole Artichokes	to serve 4

4 globe artichokes each weighing 350-400 g
Lemon juice
Salt

Twist off the stalks. Trim tough outer leaves. Cut off tops and wash thoroughly in cold running water. Rub cut surfaces with lemon juice to prevent discoloration. Put the artichokes, stalk end down, into a saucepan of boiling salted water. Add 20 ml of lemon juice. Cover the pan. Boil gently until the artichokes are tender. The time taken will vary from 25 to 45 minutes. When cooked the inner leaves will pull away easily. Drain. Serve hot with melted butter or hollandaise sauce, or serve cold with vinaigrette sauce.

Stuffed Globe Artichokes	to serve 4

Prepare and cook 4 globe artichokes as for *boiled whole artichokes*. Drain and cool. Open the leaves gently. Remove the choke with a teaspoon. Fill the central cavity of each artichoke with a savoury filling. Put the artichokes into a baking dish with 100 ml of water. Cook in a moderate oven (350°F, 175°C or mark 4) for 10 minutes.

Filling 1. Prawns and rice
100 g rice
425 ml stock
1 small onion
25 g butter or margarine
100 g chopped prawns
5 ml finely grated lemon peel
5 ml lemon juice
25 ml chopped mint
20 ml chopped parsley
Salt and pepper

Boil the rice in the stock. Chop the onion and fry it in the fat. Mix all the ingredients. Season to taste.

Filling 2. Bacon and mushrooms
4 large mushrooms
2 tomatoes
2 rashers of bacon
1 small onion
50 g butter or margarine
Salt and pepper

Chop separately the onion, bacon, mushrooms and tomatoes. Fry the onion and bacon in the butter or margarine for 5 minutes. Add the mushrooms and tomatoes. Cook for a further 5 minutes. Season to taste.

Other suggestions

First boil the whole artichoke. Remove the choke.
1 Use the artichoke as the centrepiece of a mixed salad. Fill the centre cavity with mayonnaise.
2 Strip off the leaves and use them as a salad ingredient.
3 Use the leaves as an omelette filling.
4 Chop the leaves and cook them in butter with an equal quantity of sliced par-boiled potatoes. Serve with roast beef, lamb or chicken.
5 Very small artichokes can be used as a garnish for roast or grilled meat.

ARTICHOKES (JERUSALEM)

Boiled Artichokes	to serve 4

400-600 g Jerusalem artichokes
15 ml lemon juice or vinegar
5 ml salt

Scrub the artichokes well then peel or scrape them. Put them straight into cold water containing lemon juice or vinegar to prevent browning. Cook for about 30 minutes in boiling salted water. They can be boiled in their skins and peeled when cooked. Serve the boiled artichokes with a white or cheese sauce.

Jerusalem Soup	to serve 4

1 kg Jerusalem artichokes
1 onion
2 sticks celery
Salt and pepper to taste
50 g butter or margarine
1 litre stock
½ litre milk

Peel and slice the artichokes and onion. Scrub and slice the celery. Melt the butter in a saucepan. Cook the vegetables in this for a few minutes without browning them. Add the stock and simmer until the vegetables are tender. Sieve or liquidize the soup then return it to the saucepan. Add the milk. Reheat, stirring all the the time. Season to taste.

Crumbed Artichokes	to serve 4

500 g of boiled artichokes
1 hard-boiled egg
30 ml chopped parsley
50 g white breadcrumbs
25 g butter
1 (2.5 ml) spoon salt
1 (1.25 ml) spoon pepper

Fry the breadcrumbs golden brown in the butter. Chop the egg finely or sieve. Mix the crumbs, eggs and parsley together and add salt and pepper. Slice the artichokes into a buttered dish. Sprinkle the mixture over the top. Reheat in a moderate oven (350°F, 180°C, gas mark 4).

Artichoke and Tomato Casserole	to serve 4

500 g artichokes
250 g tomatoes
1 large onion
500 ml stock
5 ml salt
2.5 ml pepper
25 g butter or margarine
20 g cornflour
5 ml dried mixed herbs
5 ml sugar
Garnish—watercress or parsley

Peel and slice the artichokes and onion. Slice tomatoes. Mix the vegetables and put them into a casserole. Blend the cornflour with a little of the stock. Melt the butter. Add the stock then the cornflour, herbs, sugar and seasoning. Pour the liquid over the vegetables in the casserole. Cook in a hot oven (400°F, 200°C or mark 6) for approximately one hour or until the vegetables are tender. Garnish. Serve with grilled gammon, roast meat or chicken.

Other suggestions
1 Thin, crisp slices eaten raw like radishes or served with a cheese dip.
2 Thick slices dipped into fritter batter and deep fried.
3 Artichoke salad made up of sliced cooked artichokes combined with a little sliced raw leek and boiled potato then marinated in a French dressing.

4 Toss slices of cooked artichokes in melted butter. Sprinkle with chopped chives or parsley.

ASPARAGUS

Basic Recipe	to serve 4

1 kg asparagus
Salt

Wash the spears carefully. Scrape them if necessary. Cut off a little of the thick white base of the stem. Tie the spears together in a neat bundle with tape. Bring a a deep pan of salted water to the boil. There should be sufficient water to reach within 3 cm of the heads when the stems are stood upright. The stems require thorough cooking while the heads need only to be steamed. Put the bundle upright in the pan. Cover and cook for about 15 minutes or until the stems are tender. Drain well. Untie the bundle. Serve the asparagus on its own with melted butter or as an accompaniment vegetable.

Asparagus Salad	to serve 4

1 bunch asparagus—about 20 stalks
500 g new potatoes
4 eggs
30 ml chopped parsley
100 ml mayonnaise
Salt and pepper
Lettuce

Cook the asparagus (see recipe above) drain well and cool. Wash the potatoes. Cook them in their skins until tender, drain and remove the skins. Hard boil the eggs for 12 minutes. Cool quickly in cold water. Remove shells. Wash and dry the lettuce. Dice the potatoes. Put them into a bowl. Cut off the tips of the asparagus and put them to one side. Cut up the rest of the stems into pieces. Add these to the potatoes. Add the chopped parsley, salt, pepper and mayonnaise to the potatoes and asparagus in the bowl. Mix gently. Arrange the lettuce around the serving dish. Put the asparagus and potato mixture into the centre.

Cut the eggs into slices or quarters and arrange these alternately with the asparagus tips around the dish.

Italian Baked Asparagus	to serve 4

500 g uncooked asparagus
4 large tomatoes
50 g butter
30 ml finely chopped onion
30 ml finely chopped celery
25 g fresh breadcrumbs
25 g grated cheese
Pinch of dried thyme
Salt and pepper

Wash and scrape the asparagus. Chop up the tomatoes. Spread the butter on the bottom of a baking dish. Arrange the asparagus spears neatly on the bottom of the dish. Spread the chopped tomatoes over them. Mix the rest of the ingredients together in a bowl and sprinkle the mixture over the asparagus and tomatoes. Cover the dish with a lid or aluminium foil. Bake in a moderately hot oven (350°F, 180°C or mark 4) for 45 minutes or until tender.

Asparagus and Eggs	to serve 4

500-700 g asparagus—fresh, frozen or canned
4 slices bread
8 eggs
Salt and pepper
Butter

Cook fresh asparagus or heat frozen or canned asparagus. Drain and keep warm. Toast the bread, butter it and lay it on a hot serving dish. Beat eggs with salt and pepper. Scramble them in butter keeping them creamy. Arrange three-quarters of the asparagus on the toast. Pour the scrambled eggs on top. Garnish with the rest of the asparagus.

Other suggestions
1 Layers of cooked asparagus alternating with sliced hard-boiled eggs set in a mould of aspic jelly. Turn out the mould on to a bed of lettuce, sliced cucumber and quartered tomatoes.
2 Serve the tips in hors-d'oeuvres, as a garnish, as an omelette filling.

3 Use asparagus stems or sprue to make cream of asparagus soup.
4 Fill pastry cases with undiluted concentrated asparagus soup, with fresh or canned asparagus tips added. Serve hot or cold.
5 Roll short lengths of asparagus in mayonnaise. Sprinkle with sieved cooked egg yolk. Serve on brown bread garnished with strips of red pepper.

AUBERGINE

Aubergine Spread	to serve 6

1 large aubergine
5 ml finely chopped onion
½ clove garlic
1 tomato
5 ml sugar
30 ml vinegar
30 ml olive oil
Salt

Peel the aubergine. Cook it in boiling salted water until tender. Peel and pulp tomato. Crush the garlic. Pound the cooked aubergine. Add all the other ingredients, blending them together until smooth. If too thick add a little more olive oil. Served chilled with toast fingers or savoury biscuits.

Stuffed Aubergine	to serve 4

2 large aubergines
1 small onion
30 ml oil
2 small sticks celery
150 g long-grain rice
3 or 4 tomatoes
50 g fresh white breadcrumbs
250 g minced beef

Cook rice in boiling salted water. Wash the aubergines, trim off stalks. Cut the aubergines in half lengthwise. Sprinkle them liberally with salt. This removes excess moisture and bitterness. Prepare and finely chop the onion. Chop the tomato and celery. Heat the oil in a saucepan. Fry the onions until soft but not brown. Add the

tomatoes and the celery and cook for a further few minutes. Add the minced beef and fry until browned all over stirring occasionally. Stir in the freshly cooked rice and season the mixture. Rinse the aubergine to remove the salt. Remove a little of the flesh from each half aubergine. Mix this in with the minced beef and rice stuffing. Put the aubergine halves into a shallow ovenproof dish. Divide the filling between the four halves. Sprinkle the breadcrumbs over them. Cover the dish and bake in a moderate oven (350°F, 180°C or mark 4) for 30 minutes. Uncover and continue cooking for a further 5 to 10 minutes until the filling is golden brown.

Moussaka	to serve 4-6

2 aubergines
2 large onions
500 g potatoes
450 g minced meat
2 tomatoes
60 ml cooking oil
1 level (2.5 ml) spoon cinnamon
1 level (2.5 ml) spoon grated nutmeg
Sauce
300 ml milk
25 g butter or margarine
25 g plain flour
1 egg
100 g cheese
Salt and pepper

Wash the sliced, unpeeled aubergines in a colander. Sprinkle them liberally with salt and leave for one hour. This removes excess moisture and bitterness.

Start to prepare the white sauce. Grate the cheese onto a plate. Melt the butter or margarine and stir in the flour gradually. Cook this slightly. Add the milk, keeping the mixture smooth. Cook over low heat, stirring all the time until the mixture thickens. Cool and stir in the egg and about half of the cheese. Do not reheat the sauce.

Peel and slice the onions, potatoes and tomatoes keeping these separated. Rinse the aubergine slices in cold water. Dry thoroughly with a clean cloth. Heat the oil in a large frying pan. Fry the aubergine slices until lightly browned on both sides then remove them and put them on a plate.

Do the same with the sliced potatoes. Fry the onions in the oil until soft, add the minced meat and turn it in the oil until it browns. Add the nutmeg and cinnamon. Arrange alternate layers of the meat, potatoes, aubergines, tomatoes and sauce in a deep casserole. Season each layer well and finish with a layer of sauce. Cover the casserole. Bake in a slow oven (325°F, 170°C, mark 3) for 1½ hours. Remove the lid. Sprinkle the top with the rest of the grated cheese then brown under the grill. Serve at once.

Ratatouille	to serve 4

2 aubergines
2 onions
15 ml chopped parsley
30-45 ml cooking oil
2 red peppers
1 baby marrow
pinch of basil
4 tomatoes
1 large clove garlic
Salt and pepper

Cut the aubergines in 2 cm cubes and put them in a colander. Sprinkle well with salt. Leave for one hour so that the excess moisture can drain off. Cut the peppers in half. Remove the centre core and the seeds. Cut the peppers into small pieces. Skin and slice the tomatoes. Cut the peeled marrow into 1 cm slices. Peel and slice the onions. Crush the garlic. Rinse the aubergines in cold water. Drain. Heat the oil in a heavy pan. Cook the onion slices until transparent. Add the aubergines, peppers and marrow. Cover and simmer for 30 minutes. Add the tomatoes, garlic, basil, salt and pepper; continue to cook for 10 minutes until the tomatoes are soft. Garnish with chopped parsley. Serve hot or cold.

Other suggestions
1 Aubergine fritters. Coat slices in batter, fry in oil. Serve sprinkled with finely chopped onion and parsley.
2 Use grilled or fried slices as a base for poached eggs or fish or small pieces of meat.
3 For aubergine salad. Peel and slice then sprinkle with salt. Leave for one hour. Rinse and dry. Sprinkle with a French dressing. Garnish with parsley.

AVOCADO PEAR

Prepare the fruit just before using. Once cut the fruit oxidizes and discolours. This can be prevented by brushing cut surfaces with lemon juice. Always use a stainless steel knife. However you intend to serve the pear, start by cutting it in half lengthwise around the stone. Carefully twist the halves to separate them. If the avocado is really ripe the stone can be removed easily with the sharp point of the knife. Avocado pears should be served at room temperature. Over-chilling spoils the texture.

Stuffed Avocado	to serve 4

2 avocado pears
Lemon juice
Lettuce
Fillings (see below)
Salt and pepper

Split the avocados and remove the stones. Brush the cut surfaces with lemon juice. Place each half on a bed of lettuce. Fill the cavity with one of the mixtures suggested below:

1 200 g cottage cheese and two sliced hard-boiled eggs.
2 Chop up two apples and two sticks of celery. Mix with mayonnaise. Sprinkle with chopped walnuts.
3 Mix 100 g sweetcorn with 100 g chopped ham. Moisten with mayonnaise.
4 Mix 15 g of cooked chicken with one chopped red pepper. Blend with mayonnaise.
5 Prawns, shrimps or crab and lettuce with French dressing.

Avocado Salads	to serve 4

1 2 avocado pears, sliced or diced
   2 heads chicory, sliced
   1 box mustard and cress
   1 lettuce
   Lemon juice
   French dressing
   Salt and pepper.

2   2 avocado pears, sliced or diced
Segments of 2 grapefruits and 2 oranges
1 lettuce
Lemon juice ⎫
10 ml sugar ⎬ shaken over the fruit
⎭
Cottage cheese (optional).

3   2 avocado pears, sliced
Lemon juice
60 g cooked chicken ⎫ mixed and blended
60 g cooked rice ⎬ with mayonnaise
⎭
Salt and pepper
Watercress or green salad.

4   2 avocado pears, sliced ⎫ Arrange in fan
4 tomatoes cut in wedges ⎬ shape on bed
⎭ of lettuce
Lettuce
Lemon juice, salt and pepper
Lemon slices, cut in butterfly shape, to garnish.

Avocado Creams	to serve 4

2 avocados
30 ml lemon juice
100 g icing sugar

Peel, halve and stone the avocados and cut them into dice. Press through a nylon sieve with the back of a wooden spoon. Stir in, a little at a time, the lemon juice. Gradually add the icing sugar. Whip until the consistency of thick cream. Spoon into chilled glasses. Decorate each with a thin slice of lemon.

Avocado and Cheese Dip	to serve 4

2 large avocado pears
30 ml lemon juice
100 g cream cheese
15 ml chopped chives or spring onions
30-50 ml milk
A few drops of oil
A few drops of Tabasco sauce

Halve, stone, skin and mash the avocado pears and mix with the lemon juice at once. Gradually blend in all the rest of the ingredients. Serve in a

bowl in the middle of a large platter. Arrange the ingredients for dipping around the bowl—small biscuits, pieces of celery, carrot slices, toast fingers.

Avocado and Mushrooms	to serve 4

1 red pepper
200 g mushrooms
25 g butter or margarine
2 avocado pears
Salt and pepper
White sauce
30 g butter or margarine
30 g flour
300 ml milk

Make the white sauce. Melt the butter, add the flour and cook without allowing it to brown. Add the milk stirring all the time. Cook gently until the sauce thickens.

Wash the mushrooms and cut into slices. Chop the pepper. Melt the butter in a frying pan and put in the chopped peppers and cook until just tender. Add the mushrooms. Cook briskly for a few minutes. Add the peppers and mushrooms to the sauce and heat through gently. Just before serving halve, stone, peel and dice the avocado pears. Add these to the hot sauce. Season to taste. Serve on buttered toast or with freshly cooked rice, noodles, spaghetti or macaroni.

Baked Sugared Avocado	to serve 4

2 avocado pears
50 g brown sugar
25 g butter
Nutmeg
Lemon juice

Butter an ovenproof dish. Peel, halve, stone and slice the avocados. Arrange the slices in the dish. Sprinkle with lemon juice and nutmeg. Spread brown sugar over the slices and dot with the rest of the butter. Bake in a fairly hot oven (375°F, 190°C or mark 5).

6

If served as a main dish or as an accompaniment to chicken or fish dishes, the baked avocado should be seasoned with salt and pepper. If used as a dessert, it can be served with fresh or soured cream.

Other suggestions
The puréed flesh of avocado may also be used to make soup or ice-cream.

BEANS

Cook very young beans whole. When the seeds have developed the beans should be shelled and only the bean seed inside used.

Basic Recipe—Broad Beans	to serve 4

400 g very young broad beans
25 g butter
Salt and pepper

Do not shell the beans. Cook them whole in boiling salted water until tender. Drain. Add the butter and salt. Toss the beans until evenly coated in melted butter.

Basic Recipe—Shelled Broad Beans	to serve 4

800 g beans
Salt and pepper

Shell the beans. Cook in boiling salted water for 15 to 20 minutes or until tender. Drain. Add pepper. Toss beans in melted butter or coat with parsley sauce. It is easier to shell tough beans after cooking.

Broad Bean Soup	to serve 4

400 g broad beans
100 g onions
1 clove garlic
50 g butter or margarine
25 g flour
½ litre stock

15 ml thyme
Salt and pepper

Shell the beans. Chop the onions and crush the garlic. Melt the butter in a saucepan and lightly fry the onion and garlic until soft but not coloured. Stir in the flour. Cook for 2 minutes. Add the stock and bring to the boil. Add the beans and thyme. Cover the pan and simmer until the beans are tender. Sieve or liquidize the soup. Add more stock if necessary to give the consistency of thin cream. Season to taste. If you wish you can add a little lemon juice or sugar. Reheat and serve.

Anglia Salad	to serve 4

300 g cooked broad beans
400 g carrots
Salt and pepper
45 ml salad cream
Shredded lettuce

Scrape, wash and grate the carrots. Put the salad cream into a bowl. Add the carrots and beans. Mix carefully until evenly coated with the dressing. Season. Pile on to a serving dish. Surround with the lettuce. Serve with cold meat.

Broad Bean Savoury	to serve 2

300 g cooked broad beans
2 tomatoes
100 g cheese
1 small onion
25 g butter or margarine
75 ml stock, tomato juice or water
Salt and pepper

Skin and slice the tomatoes. Finely chop the onion. Cube the cheese (1 cm dice). Melt the butter in a frying pan. Add the onions and cook until transparent but not coloured. Add the beans and cook gently for a few minutes. Add the liquid, salt and pepper. Cover with a lid, foil or greasproof paper. Cook gently for 5 minutes. Add the tomatoes and three-quarters of the cheese. Cook for a further 10 minutes. Add the rest of the cheese. Serve.

Other suggestions

Very tough broad beans can be used to make bean puree. Boil the beans and press them through a sieve. The tough skins will be left behind. Pour a little melted butter over the resulting puree. Serve this on hot buttered toast, scrambled eggs or with grilled bacon.

Basic Recipe—French Beans to serve 4

400-600 g French beans
25 g butter or margarine
Salt and pepper

If necessary, top and tail the beans. Leave young beans whole, large beans should be broken in two. Cook in boiling salted water for 10 to 20 minutes until just tender. Drain and toss in the melted butter. Season to taste.

French Bean Salad to serve 4

200 g cooked French beans
4 tomatoes
4 cooked potatoes
1 red pepper
Lettuce or watercress
30 ml French dressing

Slice the tomatoes, potatoes and pepper. Keep them separate. Cut the beans into short lengths. Arrange the vegetables in neat separate rows on a shallow serving dish. Pour the dressing evenly over the vegetables. Garnish with lettuce or watercress.

Beans and Yoghourt to serve 4

200 g cooked green beans
100 g mushrooms
25 g butter
1 carton yoghourt or sour cream
Salt and pepper

Chop the mushrooms. Melt the butter. Lightly cook the mushrooms for 2 to 3 minutes. Add the cooked beans, salt and pepper. Then, over low heat, stir in the yoghourt or cream. Heat through and serve.

Bean Casserole to serve 3 or 4

200 g green beans
1 small onion
¼ litre condensed mushroom soup
1 red pepper
Salt and pepper
150 ml milk

Top and tail beans. Cut into short lengths. Chop onions and red pepper. Put all the ingredients into a casserole. Bake uncovered in a moderate oven (350°F, 180°C, gas mark 4) for one hour.

Green Bean Salad to serve 4-6

400 g green beans
Salt
Lettuce
30 ml chopped parsley
Garlic dressing
90 ml oil
Juice of a lemon
Salt and black pepper
1 large clove of garlic

Top and tail the beans. Cook in boiling salted water until tender. Drain and toss with garlic dressing while still warm. Cool. Line a bowl or dish with lettuce and arrange the beans neatly in the centre. Sprinkle with chopped parsley.

Garlic dressing: combine oil and lemon juice; add the crushed garlic clove, salt and freshly ground black pepper.

Basic Recipe—Runner Beans to serve 4

400-600 g runner beans
25 g butter
Salt and pepper

Cut tips and stalks. If very young and tender leave whole, otherwise pull off tough strings from either side and cut the pod diagonally in short lengths. Cook in boiling salted water for 10 to 20 minutes. Drain and toss in melted butter. Season to taste.

BEAN SPROUTS

Bean Sprout Salad (1) — to serve 4

250 g fresh or canned bean shoots
8 sticks celery
1 box mustard and cress
60-90 ml mayonnaise or salad dressing

Rinse and drain the bean shoots and the clipped cress. Clean celery, slice thinly. Rinse and drain. Mix all the ingredients in a bowl. The mayonnaise should coat the vegetables evenly. Serve chilled.

Bean Sprout Salad (2) — to serve 4

200 g bean sprouts
1 bunch watercress
50 g salted peanuts
2 bananas
lemon juice
10 ml honey
75 ml mayonnaise
Lettuce

Rinse and drain the bean sprouts. Wash and chop the watercress. Stir the honey into the mayonnaise. Slice the bananas into a bowl. Sprinkle the slices with lemon to prevent them browning. Add the peanuts and beansprouts. Mix in the mayonnaise. Line a bowl with lettuce leaves. Put the mixture into the bowl. Sprinkle the chopped watercress over the salad.

Chinese Spring Rolls — to serve 4

200 g frozen puff pastry (thawed)
100 g chopped prawns or shrimps
Salt and pepper
Lemon juice
150 g bean sprouts
150 g chopped minced pork
Soy sauce
Vegetable oil

Mix the bean sprouts, prawns and minced pork. Season with salt and pepper, soy sauce and lemon juice. Roll out the pastry very thinly. Cut into 10 cm squares. Put some of the mixture on to each square of pastry. Damp the edges of the squares. Roll up tightly and press edges tightly to seal. Heat vegetable oil in a deep fryer. Fry golden brown. Drain well in kitchen paper.

Bean Sprouts with Mushrooms — to serve 2

400 g bean sprouts
150 g button mushrooms
1 leek or small onion
100 g chopped cooked ham
25 g butter or margarine
30 ml cornflour
15 ml soy sauce
30 ml water
Salt and pepper

Prepare and slice the onion or leek and the mushrooms. Drain the bean sprouts. Fry the onion or leek and the mushrooms in the butter. Add the water and salt. Bring to the boil. Cook for 10 minutes. Add the ham. Blend the cornflour with the soy sauce and a little water. Stir this into the mixture. Cook for one minute. Stir in the bean sprouts. Heat through and serve.

Other suggestions
1 Use the bean shoots as a sandwich filling.
2 Bean shoots can be used as an ingredient for green salads.
3 Add to cooking cabbage at the very last minute so that they are heated through but not cooked.

BEETROOT

Basic Recipe—Boiled Beetroot

Do not scrub, peel or top and tail the beetroot as it will bleed and lose colour and flavour.

Rinse the roots and cut off the leaves a little way above the roots. Cook the roots in boiling salted water until tender. Cooking time will depend on the size and age of the roots but it is usually about 2 hours. Drain. The skins should now peel off easily.

Creamed Beetroot
to serve 4

1 large or 2 small cooked beetroots
25 g butter or margarine
25 g flour
250 ml milk
Salt and pepper
Grated horseradish (optional)
30 ml vinegar

Skin and dice the beetroot (10 mm dice). Melt the butter in a saucepan and mix in the flour. Add the milk gradually and bring to the boil stirring continuously. Boil for 2 to 3 minutes. Add seasoning and vinegar. Add the cubes of beetroot to the sauce and heat until the beet is heated through and the sauce coloured pink. Dish and serve at once sprinkled with horseradish.

Dutch Beetroot
to serve 6

2 large cooked beetroots
1 large onion
50 g butter
4 cooking apples
Salt, pepper
Nutmeg
Chives

Peel and chop the beetroot. Chop the onion finely. Peel, core and chop the apples. Cook the onion in the butter until soft in a covered pan. Add the beetroot and the apple and simmer for 20 to 30 minutes until the mixture is reduced to a thick purée. Season well with salt, pepper and nutmeg. Turn into a serving dish. Sprinkle with chopped chives. Serve on its own with fried bread or as an accompaniment vegetable with meat or sausages.

Beetroot Soup
to serve 4

450 g cooked beetroot
1 litre stock
250 ml milk
25 g butter

1 onion
25 g cornflour
Seasoning
Carton (approximately 150 ml) cream or yoghourt

Slice the onion and the beetroot. Melt the butter and cook the onion until transparent but not browned. Add the beetroot, stock and seasoning. Simmer for 1 to 1½ hours. Rub through a hair sieve or liquidizer. Blend the cornflour with a little milk and add it to the soup. Bring it to the boil. Add the rest of the milk then the cream or yoghourt. Serve with fried croutons.

Beetroot and Apple Salad
to serve 4

1 medium-sized cooked beetroot
1 large cooking apple
Watercress
1 tablespoon oil
1 tablespoon vinegar
Salt and pepper

Mix oil, vinegar, salt and pepper. Peel and cut beetroot into small dice. Peel, core and roughly cut the apple. Put the apple and beetroot in a bowl and add the oil and vinegar dressing. Stir carefully. Pile on to a serving dish, garnish with watercress.

Pickled Beets
to serve 4

150 ml vinegar
130 ml water
25 g brown sugar
2.5 ml cinnamon
1.25 ml salt
1.25 ml ground cloves
450 g cooked beetroot
Cocktail onions

Dice or thinly slice the beetroot. Put all the ingredients other than the beetroot and onion, into a saucepan. Heat to boiling point. Pour over the beetroot then chill for at least 6 but preferably 12 hours. Drain and serve. Garnish with tiny pickled onions.

Beet Green with Caraway Seeds   to serve 3-4

750 g crisp beetroot leaves
25 g butter
5 ml caraway seeds
Salt and black pepper

Use only crisp bright green beetroot leaves. Wash thoroughly and put them into a shallow saucepan. Add just enough boiling water to prevent them burning. Simer for 15 minutes, stirring frequently. Add butter and caraway seeds, salt and pepper. Mix well. Serve with boiled or roast beef or bacon.

BROCCOLI

Basic Recipe   to serve 4

600-900 g broccoli
Salt

Discard the coarse leaves and stems. Cut off the flower head with about 5 cm stalk. Keep the flower sprays whole. Shred the leaves. Wash the broccoli in salted water. Cook in the minimum of boiling salted water in a closed pan for 10 to 15 minutes, or until tender. Drain thoroughly. Serve with melted butter or lemon dressing.
Broccoli can be tied in bundles and cooked like asparagus.

Broccoli Salad   to serve 4

Cooked broccoli
Cooked red peppers
Lettuce
200 ml French dressing

Chill broccoli. Cut red peppers into short strips. Shred lettuce. Arrange the broccoli on bed of shredded lettuce. Cover with dressing then garnish with pimento strips. Serve with cold meat.

Other suggestions
1 Sieve cooked broccoli to make a purée. Coat with Hollandaise sauce.

2 Mix equal quantities of pureed broccoli and white sauce. Season highly and put into a baking dish. Sprinkle with buttered crumbs or crushed cornflakes and grated cheese. Bake for 15 minutes in a moderate oven (350°F, 180°C or mark 4).

BRUSSELS SPROUTS

Basic Recipe   to serve 4

1 kg Brussels sprouts
Salt

Remove damaged outer leaves. Trim away stalks. Cut across through the base of the stalk to allow cooking water to penetrate to the middle of the sprout. Rinse in cold salted water. Cook in the minimum of boiling salted water in a pan, without a lid, for 10 to 15 minutes or until tender. Drain thoroughly. Toss in melted butter and serve immediately.

Grapefruit and Sprout Salad   to serve 4

225-350 g Brussels sprouts
150 g grapes
1 small stalk celery
100 ml French dressing
1 large grapefruit
200 g boiled potatoes
50 g split roasted almonds

Dice the potatoes. Slice the celery. Peel the grapefruit, remove white skin from each section, discard this with the pips and cut up the grapefruit flesh. De-pip the grapes. Trim, wash, and drain sprouts and slice them finely. Put the sprouts into a salad bowl. Put all the rest of the salad ingredients in, add the dressing and turn the salad.

Cream of Brussels Soup   to serve 4-6

1 kg Brussels sprouts
1 small onion

11

1 litre chicken stock (or water and 2 chicken stock
cubes)
50 g butter or margarine
35 g flour
140 ml milk or single cream
Salt and pepper

Trim and wash the sprouts. Slice, peel and finely
chop the onion. Cook the onions and sprouts in
the stock until tender, about 10 minutes. Purée in
a liquidizer or rub through a sieve. In a clean
saucepan melt the butter and blend in the flour.
Cook gently without browning for 5 minutes.
Gradually stir in the puréed sprouts. Bring to the
boil and simmer for 5 minutes. Season to taste.
Stir in the milk or cream and reheat. Serve.

Other suggestions
1 Brussels sprouts with mushrooms. Add sautéed
   mushrooms to cooked sprouts.
2 Sprouts and bacon. Fry 25 g chopped streaky
   bacon in 50 g butter. Toss in 1 kg freshly
   cooked sprouts.
3 Sprouts with almonds (or chestnuts). Cook 1 kg
   Brussels sprouts until tender but still crisp. Fry
   50 g chopped nuts in 50 g butter until golden
   brown. Pour nuts and butter over the sprouts.

CABBAGE

Basic Recipe—Boiled Cabbage   to serve 4

450-600 g cabbage
Salt

Trim off damaged leaves. Cut off stalk and wash
the cabbage in cold salted water but do not soak
it. Dry, quarter and then shred finely with a sharp
knife. Use the minimum of boiling salted water.
Put the leaves into the saucepan a handful at a
time so that the water does not go off the boil. Put
the lid on the saucepan. Cook gently for the
shortest possible time until the cabbage is tender
but crisp. It is overheating and prolonged cooking
that causes the offensive smell and loss of colour.
Drain well. Serve the cabbage immediately.

If cabbage is cooked in this way there is very little
excess liquid to drain and what there is will be
pleasantly flavoured and suitable for use in soups
or gravy.

Dolmas—Cabbage Parcels   to serve 4
---

8 large perfect cabbage leaves
Fillings: see below.
Sauce: see below.

Dip the leaves briefly in boiling water to soften
them and make them pliable. Divide the filling
into eight parts. Put each part in a cabbage leaf.
Roll this up into a neat bundle. Pack the bundles
into a casserole. Cover with sauce and cook in a
moderate oven for about one hour (350°F, 175°C
or mark 4).

Filling (1)
50 g chopped onion
50 g butter or margarine
200 g sliced mushrooms
200 g rice
750 ml stock
1 tablespoon chopped parsley
Salt and pepper

Melt the butter in a large frying pan and cook the
chopped onions. Stir in the rice; cook until
transparent. Add the mushrooms, parsley, stock,
salt and pepper. Simmer gently until the rice is
tender and has absorbed the stock.

Filling (2)
1 egg
50 g onions
100 g minced meat
30 ml stock
1 tablespoon tomato paste
¼ teaspoon grated nutmeg
Salt and pepper

Peel and chop the onion. Put in a pan with stock
and cook until tender. Add the tomato, nutmeg
and meat. Stir thoroughly. Beat the egg and add it
to the mixture.

Filling (3)
100 g chopped onion
40 g butter or margarine
300 g cream cheese
1 egg
¼ teaspoon dried thyme
1 teaspoon paprika
1 tablespoon caraway seeds

Cook onions gently in the butter. Add the rest of
the ingredients.

Sauce (1)
250 ml milk
25 g butter
50 g fresh white breadcrumbs
1 dessertspoon chopped parsley

Put all the ingredients in a saucepan. Heat until the butter melts. Beat then pour the mixture over the parcels.

Sauce (2)
75 g chopped onions
1 medium carrot diced
Medium sized can of tomatoes
1 dessertspoon vinegar
Bouquet garni
25 g brown sugar

Cook all the ingredients together for 20 minutes. Remove the bouquet garni. Pour the sauce around the parcels.

Coleslaw	to serve 4-6

There are many variations of this recipe. All consist of finely sliced cabbage mixed with a number of other finely chopped ingredients moistened by a salad dressing.

1 ½ large cabbage, shredded finely
   1 medium onion, chopped finely
   1 large carrot, grated
   25-50 g chopped walnuts
   75-90 g mayonnaise
   Salt and pepper

2 ½ large cabbage, shredded finely
   25 g sultanas
   ½ green pepper, sliced finely
   25 g chopped walnuts
   2 sticks of celery, diced
   1 carrot, grated
   60 ml French dressing
   Salt and pepper

3 *Green coleslaw*
   ½ white cabbage, shredded
   Cucumber, finely sliced
   Parsley, chopped
   Green peas, cooked
   Chives, chopped

Green pepper, finely sliced
French dressing
Salt and pepper

4 *Red coleslaw*
   ½ white cabbage, shredded
   Cucumber, peeled and diced
   Cooked beetroot, diced
   Red pepper, finely sliced
   Onion, finely chopped
   A carton of sour cream
   Salt and pepper

Cabbage Salads	to serve 4

Wash the cabbage and shred finely then mix with the other ingredients. Serve in one large salad bowl or in individual dishes. Firm white heads are particularly suitable for salads.

1 1 firm head cabbage
   50-100 g raisins
   30 ml lemon juice
   20 g sugar
   Optional—chopped nuts, dried fruit of any
      kind, chopped pineapple

2 Cabbage
   Spring onion freshly chopped
   Parsley
   Red cabbage

3 ½ head cabbage
   Onion, finely chopped
   Radishes, sliced
   Dressing of sour cream
   Horseradish, grated
   20 g sugar
   Salt

4 ½ head cabbage
   1 large cooking apple, diced
   50 g raisins or sultanas
   1 carrot, grated

5 ½ head cabbage
   2 or 3 sticks celery, finely sliced
   2 red peppers, finely sliced
   1 onion, thinly sliced
   French dressing to moisten

Basic Recipe—Red Cabbage

Follow the directions for cooking cabbage
(page 12) but add a tablespoon of vinegar or
lemon juice to the cooking water, otherwise the
colour is lost and the cabbage turns grey.

Bavarian Cabbage — to serve 6

1 large white or red cabbage
1 onion
1 cooking apple
75 g butter or margarine
25 g flour
Salt and pepper
10 ml sugar
140 ml stock or water
A few caraway seeds
70 ml white wine vinegar

Trim off the damaged outer leaves of the cabbage,
Wash, quarter and shred finely. Chop the onion
and apple finely. Melt the butter in a thick
saucepan. Fry the onion lightly. Add the cabbage,
apple, salt, pepper, caraway seeds and stock.
Cover the saucepan tightly. Simmer gently for one
hour. Sprinkle in the flour and stir. Add the wine
or vinegar. Stir and bring to the boil.

Sweet and Sour Red Cabbage — to serve 6

1 red cabbage
1 large onion
75 g redcurrant, apple or gooseberry jelly
200 ml water
5 ml salt
25 g sugar
15 ml vinegar

Finely shred the cabbage. Chop the onion finely.
Put the jelly, water, salt and sugar in a pan large
enough to take all the ingredients. When the sugar
has dissolved add the cabbage and onion. Cover
and simmer until the cabbage is tender, about 15
minutes. Remove the lid. Continue cooking gently
until the liquid has evaporated. Turn the
vegetables constantly to prevent them sticking to
the pan. Add the vinegar. Put the lid back on and
toss the vegetables to distribute the vinegar evenly.
Serve immediately while very hot. This is
particularly good with pork or ham or pork
sausages.

CARROTS

Basic Recipe—Boiled Carrots — to serve 4

400-600 g carrots
25 g butter
Salt and pepper
20 ml chopped parsley

New carrots should be cooked without scraping
first. The skins can be rubbed off when cooked.

Trim off both ends of main crop carrots and
scrape with a vegetable knife or potato peeler. Cut
carrots into strips or slices or dice.

Cook in boiling water until tender. Time will
range from 15 to 30 minutes depending on the age
of the carrots and the thickness of the pieces.
Drain well. Add the butter, salt and pepper to
taste. Toss the carrots carefully over a low heat to
coat evenly with melted butter. Turn onto a hot
serving dish and sprinkle with finely chopped
parsley.

Oven carrots — to serve 4

400 g carrots
4 spring onions
25 g butter
60 ml chopped parsley
1 (2.5 ml) spoon salt
Pinch of pepper
60 ml single cream or top of the milk

Scrape the carrots and cut in strips. Chop the
onions, including the tops. Fry the onion in the
butter. Put all the ingredients into a buttered
casserole dish. Cover and bake for 45 minutes
(350°F, 180°C or mark 4).

14

Carrot Tea Loaf

100 g self-raising flour
Pinch of salt
1 (5 ml) spoon ground cinnamon
75 g butter or margarine
1 egg
100 g grated carrot
50 g chopped walnuts
100 g sugar

Grease a 15 cm cake tin and light the oven
(375°F, 190°C or mark 5). Cream the butter or
margarine and sugar. Beat in the beaten egg. Fold
in the sieved flour, salt and cinnamon. Blend in
the carrots and walnuts. Turn into cake tin. Bake
for 45 minutes. Turn out and cool on a cooling
rack.

Carrot Salads   to serve 4

1 450 g carrots
   60 ml corn oil
   15 ml lemon juice
   25 g sugar
   1 (2.5 ml) spoon salt
   About 40 ml chopped fennel, or parsley or chives
   Watercress or lettuce

Grate the carrot very finely or cut into matchstick-
sized pieces. Mix in all the other ingredients. Chill
for at least an hour. Just before serving, drain off
all surplus liquid. Arrange on a serving dish.
Garnish with the watercress or lettuce.

2 4 large carrots
   100 g seedless raisins
   50 g chopped walnuts or peanuts

Dressing
   140 ml carton soured cream
   140 ml mayonnaise
   12 g castor sugar
   Juice and rind of small lemon
   Pinch of salt, pinch of pepper

Grate the carrot coarsely. Mix with the nuts and
raisins. Beat the dressing ingredients together and
fold through the carrot mixture. Serve in a chilled
bowl.

3 4 hard, green eating apples
   4 carrots
   60-90 ml lemon juice
   Lettuce leaves

Core the apples and grate them. Peel and grate
the carrots. Put the apples and carrots into a bowl.
Add the lemon juice and stir it in thoroughly.
Make a bed of lettuce leaves in a bowl or dish.
Arrange the carrot and apple mixture neatly in
this.

CAULIFLOWER

Basic Recipe

Whole cauliflower. Remove the coarse outer
leaves. Trim the stems and cut into the stems from
the base. Cook the head, stalk down, in boiling
salted water for 20 to 30 minutes.

Sprigged cauliflower. Break the head into
flowerets. Trim and split the stems; cook the
flowerets for 10 to 20 minutes in boiling salted
water.

Drain the cauliflower. Coat with a sauce.

Cauliflower Salad   to serve 4

1 large cauliflower
1 onion
½ cucumber
Watercress
70 ml cider or wine vinegar
70 ml salad oil
50 g castor sugar
Salt and pepper
5 ml dry mustard

Slice onions into very thin rings. Dice the
cucumber (1 cm) and soak in the vinegar for
half an hour. Blanch the cauliflower in boiling
salted water for 5 minutes. Drain, cool and sprig.
Drain the cucumber. Do not discard the vinegar.
Put the cucumber, cauliflower and onions into a

bowl. In another bowl mix together the oil, the vinegar from the cucumber, sugar, salt, pepper and mustard. Mix well. Pour this dressing over the vegetables. Turn the vegetables until they are evenly coated by the dressing. Chill. Pile neatly on to a serving dish. Garnish with the watercress.

Cauliflower Fritters   to serve 4

---

1 small head cauliflower
25 g flour
Salt, pepper
A little milk
Fat or oil for frying

Batter
75 g self-raising flour
15 ml salad oil
Pinch of salt

Divide the cauliflower into flowerets. Wash well, steam or boil until just tender but still crisp. Drain and cool. Toss the cauliflower in a little milk and then in the seasoned flour until lightly coated. To make the batter, sieve the flour and salt, and stir in the oil and just enough tepid water to give a thick creamy consistency. Heat a deep pan of oil or fat. Using a spoon, dip the cauliflower sprigs in batter, then fry for 2 to 3 minutes until puffed up and golden brown. Drain on kitchen paper. Serve hot.

Cauliflower Soup   to serve 4-6

---

1 cauliflower cut into sprigs
25 g butter or margarine
½ onion
½ litre stock
¼ litre milk
Salt and pepper

Blanch the cauliflower in boiling salted water for 5 minutes. Drain. Melt the margarine in the saucepan. Sautée the onions and cauliflower for 10 minutes. Add the stock. Bring to the boil and then simmer for 20 to 30 minutes. Rub through sieve or liquidize. Return to the saucepan. Stir in milk, season and reheat.

Cauliflower au Gratin   to serve 4

---

1 head cauliflower
25 g fresh breadcrumbs
25 g butter

Sauce
50 g butter
50 g flour
½ litre milk
100 g grated cheese
15 ml made mustard

Cook and sprig the cauliflower. Make a white sauce. Add the cheese and mustard. Put the vegetable into a greased baking dish. Pour the sauce over. Sprinkle with breadcrumbs and dot with butter. Bake in a moderate oven (350°F, 180°C or mark 4) for 20 minutes or until golden brown.

Other suggestions
The flowerets may be cooked by the Chinese stir-fry method by boiling until half cooked and then frying in a little oil.

CELERIAC

Basic Recipe   to serve 4

A celeriac root weighing about 450 g
Lemon juice or sugar

The flesh of celeriac discolours when exposed to air so should be cut just before cooking. If you are only using part of a root wrap the left over piece in foil or cling plastic for use later. The uneven root is difficult to peel so first cut it into slices. Peel thickly. Cut into slices or cubes. Cook in boiling salted water to which you have added lemon juice or vinegar to prevent discolouration of the flesh. Cook until tender, 15 to 20 minutes. Serve plain with butter, salt and pepper.

Celeriac Pie   to serve 4

---

200 g cooked celeriac
200 g cooked potatoes
100 g cooked ham
1 egg
A pinch of nutmeg
25 g butter

Slice the celeriac. Put this neatly at the bottom of
an oven-proof dish. Cover with slices of cooked
ham. Mash the potatoes with the butter, egg and
nutmeg. Spread the potatoes over the ham and
cook in a moderate oven (350°F, 180°C or mark 4)
until golden brown and crisp on top.

Other suggestions

1 *Celeriac fritters*. Slice cooked celeriac thinly, dip
  in flour, then batter, and deep fry.
2 Coat hot cooked slices of celeriac with a cheese
  sauce. Brown in the oven or under a grill.
3 *Baked celeriac*. Scrub the root, cut it in half and
  bake until tender (for about one hour) in a
  moderate oven. Serve with salt, pepper and
  butter.
4 Blanch the celeriac slices and then stew them in
  stock with butter.
5 Serve celeriac raw, grated in salad or stirred into
  a mayonnaise.

CELERY

Celery Soup   to serve 4

---

200 g chopped celery
100 g chopped onion
100 g chopped potato
75 g butter or margarine
1 litre chicken stock
Salt and pepper
20 ml cream (optional)

Melt the butter in a saucepan. Cook the celery,
onion and potato in the melted butter for about 10
minutes. The vegetables should not be allowed to
brown. Add the stock. Cover and simmer for 40
minutes, or 20 minutes if you have a liquidizer.

Sieve or liquidize the soup. Season to taste.
Reheat. Stir a little cream into each bowl of soup
before serving.

Braised Celery   to serve 4

---

1 large head celery
50 g butter or margarine
Chopped parsley
1 (2.5 ml) spoon salt
1 (1.25 ml) spoon pepper
15 ml water

Clean the celery and cut it into 7 to 10 cm
lengths. Melt the butter in a casserole. Roll the
celery in the butter and add the seasoning and the
water. Cover and bake in a moderate oven (350 F,
180°C or mark 4) for 1¼ hours. Serve sprinkled
with chopped parsley.

Celery Salads   to serve 4

---

1 *Celery, apple and beetroot*. Combine 8 chopped
  celery sticks with 2 diced eating apples and a
  medium-sized grated beetroot. Mix with a little
  French dressing and serve with watercress.

2 *Celery and walnuts*. A head of celery trimmed,
  washed and sliced, plus half its weight in
  chopped nuts. Mix with 90 ml of mayonnaise.
  Chill and garnish with watercress.

3 *Celery and fennel*. A head of celery trimmed,
  washed and sliced mixed with one head, sliced,
  of fennel. Moisten with French dressing.
  Garnish with 50 to 75 g cheese, grated or diced.

Other suggestions
1 *Celery and sprouts*. Add chopped celery to
  cooking sprouts about 7 minutes before they are
  ready.
2 Cut celery into neat 10 cm sticks to be served
  with a cheese dip.
3 Cut celery into 4 cm lengths. Fill the channel
  with: (a) a mixture of four parts grated cheese
  to one of butter, plus salt and pepper; or
  (b) unsalted butter sprinkled with sea salt.
4 *Celery parcels*. Parboil the celery. Stretch
  streaky bacon rashers and wrap them around

the sticks. Put them in a baking dish. Bake in a moderate oven for 30 minutes. Garnish with grilled tomatoes and parsley.

5 The feathery tops are strongly flavoured and are excellent in soups.

CELTUCE

Celtuce Salad	to serve 4

4 stems of celtuce
2 dessert apples
1 small, crisp cabbage
10 radishes
Juice of ½ lemon
200 g cottage cheese
30 ml French dressing
Salt and pepper

Peel the apples. Chop the apples and celtuce into small pieces. Sprinkle with the lemon juice. Turn the cottage cheese into a bowl and add the seasoning. Beat lightly. Fold in the celtuce and apples. Wash, dry and finely shred the cabbage. Toss in French dressing until evenly coated. Arrange the cabbage in a serving dish. Pile the cheese and vegetables in the centre. Garnish with radishes.

Celtuce Casserole	to serve 4

6 stems of celtuce
40 g butter
Salt and pepper
15 ml chicken stock

Cut the celtuces into 4 cm pieces. Wash and drain. Using part of the butter, grease an ovenware dish. Put the celtuce, stock, seasoning and the rest of the butter in the dish. Cover. Cook for about one hour in a moderate oven (350°F, 180°C or mark 4). Serve with meat or poultry dishes.

Other suggestions
Use recipes suggested for lettuce and celery.

CHARDS

The outer leaves cook like spinach, the white stalks or chards can be tied in bundles and cooked like seakale or asparagus. Strip the leaves from the stalks. Wash and drain well. Wash the stalks in cold water with lemon juice.

Swiss Chard Leaves	to serve 4

700 g chard leaves
15 ml olive oil or corn oil
Salt and black pepper

Wash the leaves and break them up into small pieces. Put the oil in a large shallow pan. Add the leaves and salt. Cook about 12 minutes turning the leaves occasionally. Drain off the surplus liquid. Sprinkle with black pepper. Serve with grills, roast meat and egg dishes.

Steamed Swiss Chards	to serve 4

350 g chards (stems)
50 g butter
5 ml salt
Black pepper

Place the prepared chards in a steamer, cover with boiling water. Sprinkle with salt. Cover and cook for 50 to 60 minutes, turning the chards occasionally. Place in a hot dish. Pour melted butter over the chards. Dust with fresh ground black pepper. Serve as a first course or with grilled meats.

CHICORY

If you intend to serve chicory cut up, prepare it very shortly before serving. Chicory has a high water content and tends to 'bleed' readily. Delay in serving could result in the vegetable being limp and watery.

Basic Recipe	to serve 4

8 heads chicory
10 ml sugar

50 g butter or margarine
Juice of a lemon
Chopped parsley

Prepare immediately before cooking. Do not soak. Remove discoloured leaves and rinse the heads under the cold tap. Dry in a clean cloth. Remove the tiny core which can taste bitter. Put the chicory in a large saucepan with 10 ml sugar, the juice of a lemon, and a little boiling water. Cover and simmer for 20 to 30 minutes until the chicory is tender but crisp. Drain well. Melt butter in the pan and roll the chicory heads in it. Sprinkle with chopped parsley.

Chicory is used raw for salads or sandwiches.

Chicory au Gratin	to serve 4

8 heads of chicory
100 g grated cheddar cheese
Salt and pepper

Sauce
50 g butter
50 g flour
¼ litre milk

Boil the chicory. Drain it and put it in a shallow baking dish. Make a white sauce. Add the cheddar cheese, salt and pepper. Pour the sauce over the chicory. Cook in a fairly hot oven (375°F, 190°C or mark 5) until the sauce is golden brown on top.

Chicory Pie	to serve 4

8 boiled heads chicory
350 g minced beef
2 onions, finely chopped
25 g dripping or margarine
Salt and pepper
Parsley

Melt the fat. Brown the finely chopped onion. Add the minced meat and mix well with the onions cooking all the time. Add the salt, pepper and parsley. Take a heatproof dish, put in a layer of four heads of chicory. Cover this with the meat and onion. Top this with the rest of the chicory. Cook in a moderate oven (350°F, 180°C or mark 4)

until golden brown. Serve with grated cheese or a savoury sauce.

Chicory Salads	to serve 4

1 4 heads chicory, sliced
   50 g chopped walnuts
   2 eating apples, diced
   50 g raisins
   100 g cheese, diced
   French dressing or mayonnaise, or cream
      seasoned with mustard and lemon juice.

Soak the raisins for one hour in warm water. Drain the raisins. Mix all the ingredients. Chill and serve.

2 4 heads chicory
   2 oranges
   Watercress

Wash the chicory and separate out the leaves. Peel oranges, cut in slices. Mix the chicory and oranges in a bowl. Garnish with watercress.

3 2 heads chicory
   340 g sweetcorn kernels
   225 g cheese
   1 small cucumber
   Watercress
   Sliced gherkins

Wash and thinly slice the chicory heads. Dice the cheese. Wash but do not peel the cucumber. Chop roughly. Mix the sweetcorn, cheese and cucumber. Line a platter with the chicory. Pile the sweetcorn mixture on to this. Garnish with the watercress and gherkins.

CHINESE CABBAGE

Basic Recipes	to serve 4

1 Wash, dry and shred cabbage. Cook in the minimum of salted water for about five minutes. Drain well. Serve with soy or tomato sauce.

2 *Chinese stir-fry method.* Wash, dry and shred the cabbage. Cover the base of a large frying pan with a thin layer of corn oil or lard. Heat.

Put in half the cabbage and stir about for 3 minutes. Add a little salt and the rest of the cabbage. Cook for another 3 or 4 minutes until all the cabbage is cooked but still slightly crisp.

3 *Sweet-sour cabbage.* Mix 50 g sugar, 20 ml wine vinegar, 50 g cornflour with 120 ml water. Add this to the cabbage when you add the salt. Stir until the cabbage is cooked and coated with the transparent sauce.

Chinese Cabbage Salad

Shred the cabbage finely and use in salads instead of lettuce or for any of the cabbage salad recipes on page 12.

Stuffed Chinese Cabbage

Follow the recipes for Dolmas on page 12.

CUCUMBER

Basic Recipe

If the cucumber is young and tender it does not have to be peeled. Some people find the skin of older cucumbers difficult to digest so it is sensible to peel them. Slice the cucumber finely for salads and sandwiches. Sprinkle the slices with salt and leave for half an hour. Tip off the resulting liquid. Dry on absorbent kitchen paper.

To cook. Blanch in boiling water for 2 to 3 minutes. Drain and return to the saucepan with a little butter, salt and pepper. Cover and cook for a few minutes until tender.

Cold Cucumber Soup   to serve 6

1 large cucumber
50 g butter

3 spring onions or one onion, chopped
800 ml stock
Sprig of mint
Salt and pepper
Grated nutmeg
10 ml arrowroot
60 ml cream

Peel and thinly slice the cucumber. Save a dozen slices for garnish. Melt butter in a saucepan. Add the cucumber. Cook over gentle heat for a few minutes. Remove the cucumber slices with a draining spoon. Put them on a plate. Add the chopped onion to the remaining butter and cook for a few minutes. Return the cucumber to the pan. Add stock and mint and bring to the boil. Cover the pan and simmer for 10 minutes. Sieve or liquidize the soup. Rinse out the pan and put the soup back into it. Season to taste. Add nutmeg. Blend the arrowroot with a little of the cream. Stir this into the soup. Bring the soup to the boil and cook for half a minute stirring all the time. Add the remaining cream. Put the soup in a bowl. Allow to cool before putting it into a refrigerator to chill. Serve soup garnished with the reserved cucumber slices.

Baked Cucumbers   to serve 4

2 thick cucumbers 20 cm long
30 ml wine vinegar
5 ml salt
Pinch of sugar
25 ml butter
5 ml chopped parsley
15 ml spring onions, chopped
Ground black pepper

Peel the cucumber and cut in half lengthwise. If the seeds are large scoop them out and discard them. Cut the cucumber in strips 1 cm wide and 5 cm long. Put the cucumber into a bowl with the vinegar, salt and sugar. Leave for 1 to 2 hours. Drain thoroughly. Put the cucumber into a baking dish with the rest of the ingredients. Mix them well. Bake uncovered in a fairly hot oven (375°F, 190 C or mark 5) until tender but still firm, for about 25 minutes.

<table>
<tr><td>**Cucumber au Gratin**</td><td>to serve 4</td></tr>
</table>

Prepare baked cucumbers (see previous recipe). Cover with thin slices of tomato. Over this pour ¼ litre of cheese sauce. Sprinkle with fresh white breadcrumbs and grated cheese. Grill for 4 to 5 minutes until golden brown.

<table>
<tr><td>**Cucumber Salads**</td><td>to serve 4</td></tr>
</table>

To prepare cucumbers for salads sprinkle the cucumber pieces with salt. Leave to drain in colander for one hour. Pat dry in a cloth or paper towel. Then proceed according to the recipe.

1 1 large cucumber
   10 ml salt
   2 cloves garlic
   2 cartons natural yoghourt
   Pepper
   Paprika
   15 ml chopped mint

Prepare the cucumber. Crush the garlic and mix it with the yoghourt, salt and pepper and 10ml of chopped mint in a bowl. Fold in the cucumber. Cover the bowl with a lid, foil or plastic. Chill. Immediately before serving sprinkle paprika and the remaining chopped mint over the salad.

2 1 cucumber
   10 ml salt
   Chopped chives
   75 g cream cheese
   15 ml lemon juice
   Black pepper

Prepare the cucumber. Beat together the cheese, lemon and black pepper. Fold in the cucumber. Sprinkle with the chopped chives.

3 1 cucumber, sliced
   4 tomatoes
   Lettuce leaves
   Chives or parsley
   Black pepper

Prepare the sliced cucumber. Slice the tomatoes thinly. Tear the lettuce into strips, and arrange the strips on a flat dish. Arrange rows of tomatoes and cucumber slices neatly on this. Sprinkle with black pepper. Sprinkle with chopped parsley or chives.

ENDIVE

Discard outer leaves, especially those which are unbleached, as they are bitter and coarse. Wash the leaves carefully as dirt tends to get trapped in the creases. Shake dry. The leaves are useful for winter salads, and may be braised or cooked like spinach. Add a teaspoon of sugar to the cooking water to minimize bitterness and bring out the flavour.

FENNEL

<table>
<tr><td>**Braised Fennel**</td><td>to serve 4</td></tr>
</table>

4 bulbs fennel
50 g butter
20 g chopped onions
Sauce
150 ml stock
25 g flour
10 ml chopped parsley
2 tomatoes, chopped
50 g grated cheese

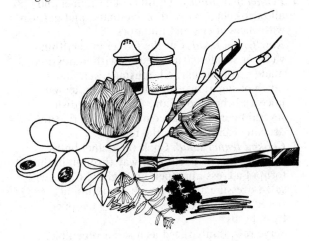

Remove tough outer leaves of the fennel. Cut the bulbs in half. Melt half the butter in a saucepan. Cook the onions for 2 to 3 minutes. Add the fennel, cover and braise until it is really cooked, about 30 to 35 minutes. Lift out the fennel and put it on to a serving dish, keep it hot.

Make a sauce with the stock. Mix the flour with the rest of the butter and some of the stock from the braised fennel. Pour this into a pan and stir

21

until the stock thickens. Add the parsley, cheese and tomato. Pour this sauce over the fennel bulbs.

Braised fennel cooked this way looks attractive served in a ring of rice.

Fennel with Onions	to serve 4

4 fennel bulbs
4 onions
¼ litre cheese sauce
2 tomatoes

Prepare the fennel and onions. Cook them whole in salted water. Drain thoroughly. Slice the fennel and onion separately. Grease an oven dish and put half the onion slices around the edge and half the fennel in the centre. For the second layer reverse the arrangement. Chop up the tomatoes. Put them into the cheese sauce. Pour this over the vegetables. Cook in a moderate oven for 20 minutes.

Other suggestions

1 *Fennel mayonnaise.* Drain cooked fennel and allow to cool. Coat with mayonnaise and garnish with slices of egg and tomatoes.
2 *Raw fennel salad.* Cut the fennel in very thin slices or slender strips. Season with a dressing made up of vinegar, oil, mustard, salt and a pinch of sugar, or with a little cream, lemon juice and chopped onion. Prepare the dish several hours in advance of serving so that the dressing can penetrate the fennel.
3 *Cooked fennel salad.* Cook the fennel bulbs whole. Drain well, cut half-way through in the form of a cross and open up slightly. Cover with salad dressing and then with a mixture of sieved hard-boiled eggs and mixed chopped fresh herbs.
4 Serve raw, thinly sliced as a salad vegetable.
5 Fennel can be made into a soup or a purée for invalids.
6 The stems and feathery leaves may be used to flavour fish sauces and soups.

GLOBE ARTICHOKE, see *Artichoke, Globe*

JERUSALEM ARTICHOKE, see *Artichoke, Jerusalem*

KOHL RABI

Allow 1 to 2 heads per person. The leaves can be cooked in the same way as spinach. The swollen stem should be cooked before peeling as the flavour is just under the skin. It can be boiled like a root vegetable and served hot with white sauce. It can be steamed, allowed to cool, then sliced and served with mayonnaise. All recipes given for turnip and celeriac may be used for this vegetable.

LAMB'S LETTUCE

A useful winter salad plant. Use instead of watercress or lettuce, on its own or as one of a mixture of salad plants. It goes particularly well with potato salad. Wash thoroughly to remove grit. Shake dry. Serve with French dressing.

LEEKS

Leeks must be washed thoroughly to remove all trace of grit. Trim off the roots, outer leaves, and top leaves as necessary. Wash in cold water. If the leeks are to be cooked whole put them, root end up, in a jar of cold salted water for at least half an hour. If they are to be cut into pieces, first split the leeks lengthwise down the middle. Wash them in salted water. Slice as required, then put the slices in a colander and rinse them thoroughly. Boil in salted water for 20 to 30 minutes or braise in a moderate oven for 1 to 1½ hours.

Braised Leeks with Bacon	to serve 4

8 medium or 12 small leeks
50 g butter or margarine
250 ml chicken stock
Salt and freshly ground black pepper
90 g bacon

Clean the leeks. Boil in salted water for 20 minutes. Drain. Butter a shallow baking dish generously. Lay the leeks in the dish. Dot the leeks with the remaining butter. Pour over the chicken stock. Season to taste with salt and pepper. Braise in a moderate oven (350°F, 180°C or mark 4). Grill the bacon. Cut it into small pieces. Sprinkle these over the leeks and serve immediately.

Cornish Leek Pie	to serve 4

350 g boiled, sliced leeks
50 g butter
125 g shortcrust pastry
100 g bacon
250 ml milk
2 eggs
Salt and pepper

Melt the butter in a saucepan. Add the leeks and cook them gently in a covered pan for 10 minutes. Cut up the bacon in to 1 cm wide strips. Mix the bacon and leeks then turn them into a pie-dish about 20 cm in diameter and 4 cm deep. Mix the milk, eggs, salt and pepper. Pour this over the leeks. Roll out the pastry to fit the dish and lay it over the leeks. Brush with milk. Bake for 20 to 30 minutes in a moderate oven (350°F, 180°C or mark 4).

Welsh Leeks	to serve 4

8 medium-sized leeks
8 rashers streaky bacon
25 g butter or margarine
Salt and pepper
Topping
50 g butter
75 g breadcrumbs
100 g grated cheese

Trim and clean the leeks thoroughly. Cut into 15 cm lengths. Rinse again and stand in boiling salted water for 10 minutes. Drain well. Remove the rind and gristle from the bacon. Wrap a rasher of bacon around each leek. Butter an ovenproof dish. Arrange the leeks and bacon neatly in rows in the dish. Season with salt and pepper. To make the topping, melt the butter and mix in the bread crumbs and cheese. Sprinkle this over the leeks. Bake in a moderate oven (350 F, 180°C or mark 4) for 40 to 50 minutes until the leeks and the topping are golden. Serve with mashed potatoes.

Leek and Potato Soup	to serve 6

1 kg potatoes
½ kg leeks
1 stick celery
1 medium onion
Salt and pepper
25 g butter
¾ litre chicken or vegetable stock
½ litre milk
140 ml single cream (optional)

Trim and clean the leeks. Slice and rinse again. Wash and chop the celery. Peel and slice the onion. Peel and slice the potatoes. Melt the butter in a large saucepan. Add the prepared vegetables. Stir the vegetables over gentle heat until the butter has been absorbed but without browning vegetables. Add the stock, salt and pepper. Simmer for half an hour or until the vegetables are tender. Sieve or liquidize the vegetables. Return the soup to the saucepan. Add the milk. Reheat but do not boil. Check the seasoning and add the cream just before serving.

LETTUCE
In this country lettuces are generally served raw although they can be braised, included in the ingredients for vegetable stews, and made into soup. They should be handled gently as they bruise easily.

Lettuce in Salads

Discard any discoloured or damaged leaves. Separate the lettuce leaves. Wash them carefully. Dry the leaves in paper towels, clean linen towels or a salad basket. If the leaves are wet, dressings will not coat the leaves but just run off them. Break the lettuce by hand into suitably sized pieces. Avoid using a knife as this might bruise the leaves and make them bitter. Salads may be made of lettuce alone, or mixed with other green vegetables, salad vegetables or vegetables and fruit. The salad dressing will vary according to the ingredients but unless the recipe states otherwise it should be added immediately before serving. If salad leaves are left soaking in a dressing they are likely to become soggy and discoloured.

Lettuce Sandwiches

Lettuce leaves
Brown bread
Butter
Finely grated lemon rind
Salt and pepper

Wash and dry the lettuce leaves. Tear the lettuce into bite-sized pieces. Season them with salt, pepper and grated lemon rind. Butter the bread. Sandwich the lettuce thickly between the bread and butter. Do not allow any lettuce to protrude from the sandwich as it becomes limp very quickly.

Quick Lettuce Soup   to serve 4

2 small lettuces
½ litre chicken stock
¾ litre milk
Salt and pepper
A pinch of sugar
A pinch of nutmeg
Chopped parsley
A little cream (optional)

Boil the stock. Add the lettuce leaves and simmer for 10 minutes. Sieve or liquidize and then return the soup to the saucepan. Add sugar, nutmeg and milk. Season to taste. Reheat and serve hot, or serve chilled. Garnish with cream and parsley.

MARROW

Use baby or middle-sized marrows for cooking. Large woody marrows can be used for preserving. There is no English name for baby marrows so we have adopted the French name *courgette*, and the Italian *Zucchini*. Small marrows or courgettes need to be simply topped and tailed leaving the peel on. They can be cooked whole if small. Larger marrows need to be peeled thickly. Cut them in half lengthwise and remove the seeds, then cut into suitable sized pieces according to the recipe. The still closed marrow flowers may be made into

fritters by dipping in batter and deep-frying and the open flowers stuffed with a savoury mixture and baked or deep-fried.

Baked Stuffed Marrow   to serve 4

1 medium-sized marrow or about
600 g baby marrows
Stuffing
See below

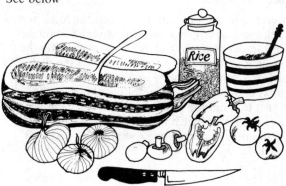

Medium-sized marrows. Prepare by washing and then removing a slice lengthwise from the marrow. Reserve this for a lid. Scoop out the seeds. Fill the hollow with stuffing, replace the marrow lid. Put the marrow in a baking dish. Bake the marrow in a moderate oven (350°F, 180°C, or mark 4) until the marrow is soft.

Marrow slices. Cut slices of marrow 5 to 8 cm thick. Scoop out the seeds. Arrange the slices in a baking dish. Fill the hollows with stuffing.

Baby marrows. Prepare by washing, then remove the seeds either by coring them from each end with an apple corer, or by cutting them in half lengthwise and scooping out the seeds. Fill the hollow with stuffing. Put halves together. If necessary hold the halves together with skewers. Bake in a moderate oven until the marrow is soft.

Suggestions for stuffing
1 300 g minced cooked meat
   100 g sliced mushrooms
   1 small onion, finely chopped
   25 g butter or margarine
   Salt and pepper

Melt the butter or margarine. Fry the onion for 3 or 4 minutes. Do not brown. Add the mushrooms. Cook for a few minutes until just soft. Stir in the meat, salt and pepper.

2 150-200 g shelled peas
   2 or 3 ripe tomatoes
   1 medium-sized green pepper
   1 medium-sized red pepper
   Salt and pepper
   Small head celery
   50 g rice
   50 g butter or margarine
   Chicken stock

Prepare the marrow. Sprinkle both halves with salt until the vegetables are ready. Peel and chop the tomatoes. Seed and chop the peppers and chop the celery. Put the peas, tomatoes, peppers and celery in a saucepan with just enough stock to come to the top of the vegetables. Bring to the boil and simmer for 5 minutes. Strain the vegetable and chicken stock into another saucepan. Bring it to the boil, add the rice and boil for 10 to 20 minutes (depending on the type of rice) until the rice is tender. Strain off any liquid, then add the vegetables to the rice. Mix well and season. Drain the marrow halves. Stuff the marrow. Bake until the marrow is tender.

Buttered Baby Marrows to serve 4

---

600 g baby marrows
40 g butter
Salt
15 ml oil
A little lemon juice

Wipe the baby marrows with a damp cloth. Top and tail them. Cut slanting 10 mm slices into a colander sprinkling each layer with salt. Cover and leave to drain for one hour. Drain off excess liquid and pat the slices dry with a clean cloth or paper towels. Heat the butter and oil in a large frying pan. Add the sliced marrow and stir lightly to coat with the melted butter and oil. Cover and cook over gentle heat for 10 minutes. Transfer to a casserole and cook for a further 10 minutes in a moderate oven. Sprinkle lightly with lemon juice. This is excellent served with roast chicken. If you like you can cook a small onion finely chopped in the melted butter and oil before cooking the marrow slices and add four chopped tomatoes before baking.

Courgette Salads to serve 4

---

1 600-800 g small baby marrows
   Parsley to garnish
   Salt, pepper, sugar
   Juice of ½ lemon
   90 ml oil

Trim stalk ends but do not peel the marrows. Boil in salted water until just tender. Mix the oil, lemon juice, salt, pepper and 5 ml sugar. Slice the marrows into this dressing. Cool. Serve chilled garnished with chopped parsley.

2 600-800 g baby marrows
   Cream cheese or mayonnaise

Thinly slice or cube the raw marrow. Mix this in with the mayonnaise or cream cheese.

3 Thinly slice the marrow and serve it with a variety of vegetables or fruit.

MUSHROOMS
Before using mushrooms for any recipe they should be wiped with a damp cloth or rinsed under a cold tap then dried thoroughly with a clean cloth or paper towel. Do not peel cultivated mushrooms.

Cream of Mushroom Soup

---

200 g mushrooms
1 small onion
350 ml chicken stock
400 ml milk
25 g butter or margarine
25 g flour
Salt and pepper
300 ml cream or top of the milk

Peel and slice the onion. Slice the mushrooms. Put the onion, mushrooms and stock in a saucepan. Bring to the boil. Cover and simmer for 20 to 30 minutes. Rub the soup through a sieve or liquidize. Melt the fat in a saucepan, add the flour and cook for one minute. Blend in the milk and add the vegetable purée. Bring to the boil stirring all the time. Simmer for 5 to 10 minutes. Pour into serving bowls and stir in a little cream or top of the milk.

Potato and Mushroom Pie — to serve 4

½ kg new potatoes
300-350 g mushrooms
75 g butter
1 large clove garlic, chopped
Salt and pepper
250 ml milk
A little cream (optional)
75 g grated cheese

Scrape the potatoes. Slice them thinly. Spread an ovenproof dish with butter. Sprinkle garlic on this. Arrange the potatoes, mushrooms and seasoning in layers, finishing with potatoes. Pour milk over the vegetables. Sprinkle with grated cheese and dot with the remaining cheese. Bake for 1½ hours in a cool oven (325°F, 170°C or mark 3) until golden brown.

Devilled Mushrooms on Toast — to serve 4

200 g mushrooms, sliced
75 g butter
4 thick slices buttered toast
5 ml Worcestershire sauce
5 ml soy sauce
Large pinch of cayenne pepper
Large pinch of salt
Lemon juice

Melt the butter, add all the seasoning. Add the sliced mushrooms, making sure they are well coated with the sauce. Cover with a lid and cook for 2 to 3 minutes. Serve with the sauce on the buttered toast.

Stuffed Mushrooms — to serve 4

16 large flat open mushrooms
45 ml corn oil
75 g butter
20 ml chopped parsley
1 large onion
100 g fresh white breadcrumbs
5 ml beef or vegetable extract
Juice and grated rind of a lemon
75-100 g grated cheese

Butter a large baking dish. Skin and finely chop the onion. Remove the mushroom stalks and chop them finely. Heat the rest of the butter and the oil in a frying pan. Fry the mushrooms quickly until the outsides are tender but the centres still uncooked. Put them gill side up on the buttered dish. Fry the onions until tender. Add the chopped mushroom stalks and breadcrumbs and fry until golden brown. Take the pan off the heat. Mix in the parsley, lemon, seasoning, beef or vegetable extract and half of the cheese. Spoon the mixture on to the mushroom centres. Top with the rest of the cheese. Bake in a moderate oven (350°F, 180°C or mark 4) for about 20 minutes or until the mushrooms are tender.

Raw Mushroom Salads — to serve 4

1 400 g sliced button mushrooms
   5 ml finely chopped chives
   5 ml finely chopped parsley
   100 ml olive or salad oil
   Juice of a lemon
   Salt and freshly ground black pepper

Pour the mixed oil and lemon juice over the sliced mushroom in a salad bowl. Toss carefully and chill for at least 30 minutes before serving. Sprinkle with salt and pepper and with the chives and parsley.

2 200 g mushrooms
   400 g tomatoes
   60 ml French dressing
   5 ml chopped fresh herbs

Wash and slice the mushrooms. Skin and slice the tomatoes. Put them in a shallow dish and pour the dressing over them. Sprinkle with herbs and leave for half an hour before serving.

3 200 g button mushrooms
   1 lettuce
   ½ chopped red pepper
   2 hard-boiled eggs
   100 ml French dressing

Slice the mushrooms. Pour the dressing over the mushrooms. Leave to stand in a refrigerator for one hour. Line a dish with lettuce leaves. Strain the dressing from the mushrooms and put them in the centre of the dish. Sprinkle the chopped pepper on top. Slice the eggs and use them to encircle the mushrooms.

Other suggestions
1 Put fried mushrooms at the bottom of ramekin or cocotte dishes. Top them with cream and eggs and seasoning. Bake for 15 minutes in a moderate oven.
2 Add chopped button mushrooms to white sauces to be served with fish or chicken.
3 Include button or flat mushrooms with ingredients for kebabs.
4 Add chopped cooked mushrooms to creamed fish.
5 Add sliced mushrooms to the meat for shepherds pie.
6 When making Welsh rarebit, top the cheese mixture with mushrooms before cooking under the grill.
7 Fill omelettes with cooked mushrooms.

MUSTARD AND CRESS
Use as a sandwich filling on its own or mixed with chopped egg or fish paste. It can be used as a garnish or as a salad ingredient, or added to a butter sauce for cooked meat.

OKRA OR LADIES FINGERS

Basic Recipe	to serve 4

12 Okras

Wash and drain. Cut off the stalk end. Leave whole or slice in rings 1 cm thick. Boil the whole pods for 10 minutes, boil sliced for 6 minutes, in boiling salted water.

Fried Okra	to serve 4

12 Okras
1 egg
Raspings (browned breadcrumbs)
Salt and pepper
Fat or oil for frying

Dip the okras in egg and roll in seasoned raspings. Fry quickly in hot fat or oil for 5 to 8 minutes. Drain and serve very hot.

Stewed Okra	to serve 4

12 okras, cut in rings
2 tomatoes, chopped
1 onion, sliced
Salt and pepper
5 ml Tabasco sauce
25 g butter

Heat the butter in a frying pan. Brown the onion and okras, stirring all the time. Add the tomatoes. Season with salt and pepper. Cook over low heat for about half an hour, stirring until the mixture thickens and the vegetables are tender. Stir in the Tabasco sauce just before serving.

Cornmeal and Okra Cake	

250 g fresh okras
350 ml water
5 ml salt
125 g yellow cornmeal
25 g butter

Wash the okras. Scrape skin lightly to remove surface fuzz. Trim off stalk at end of pod. Thinly slice crosswise. Put the okras, salt and water into a pan. Bring to the boil. Put on the lid, lower the heat and simmer for 10 minutes until the okra is tender. Pour the cornmeal in a thin stream stirring all the time. Cook over a gentle heat, stirring all the time for 5 minutes or until the mixture is thick enough to leave the bottom and sides of the pan to form a solid mass. Spoon into a heated serving dish to make a round cake about 2 cm deep and 20 cm in diameter. Spread the top with softened butter and serve at once as an accompaniment to fish or meat.

ONIONS
To peel an onion use a very sharp vegetable knife. Cut off the roots. Remove the papery brown skin and one outer layer of the onion. Trim off the top. Small onions are more easily peeled if they are

topped and tailed then immersed in boiling water for 2 minutes. To chop an onion efficiently cut it in half and place the flat surfaces on the chopping board. Cut in thin slices across. Cut down the slices to make strips, then cut across the strips to make small pieces. This method keeps the juices intact. Rinse hands and equipment in cold water before washing in hot water so as to ensure removal of the smell. Onions, if they are to be cooked whole or other than for flavouring, must be blanched. Put them in cold water, bring to the boil and cook for 2 minutes. Drain the onions which are now ready for further cooking.

French Onion Soup — to serve 4-6

4 large Spanish onions
100 g butter
25 g sugar
1½ litre beef stock or water (or a mixture of stock and water)
Salt and freshly ground black pepper
Toasted rounds of French bread
Butter
Grated gruyère cheese

Peel and slice onions thinly. Separate the rings. Heat the butter in a large saucepan with the sugar. Add the onion rings. Cook them very gently over a very low heat stirring constantly until they are an even pale golden brown. Add the beef stock gradually, stirring constantly until the soup comes to the boil. Lower the heat and cover the pan. Simmer gently for 30 minutes. Check the seasoning. Butter the rounds of toast and heap them with the cheese. Put these into a tureen or individual soup bowls and pour the soup over them.

Onion Flan — to serve 4-6

Shortcrust pastry
200 g flour
100 g mixed lard and margarine
Cold water
Pinch of salt
Filling
2 large onions
140 ml milk
75 g grated cheese
1 egg
Salt, pepper, parsley

Make the pastry and line a 20 cm flan ring, pie plate or sandwich tin. Peel the onions. Slice thinly then cook in boiling water until soft. Drain well. Mix the onions, egg, milk, 50 g cheese, salt and pepper. Pour this into the pastry case and sprinkle on the rest of the cheese. Bake in a fairly hot oven (400°F, 200°C or mark 6) for 10 minutes. Reduce the temperature to moderate (350°F, 180°C or mark 4). Cook for a further 25 to 30 minutes until the filling is set and golden brown and the pastry cooked through. Serve hot or cold garnished with parsley.

Welsh Onion Pie — to serve 4

1 kg potatoes
½ kg onions
100 g grated cheddar cheese
10 g butter or margarine
Salt and pepper

Peel, blanch and chop the onions. Peel and thinly slice the potatoes. Butter a pie-dish and then arrange alternate layers of potatoes, onions and cheese and seasoning. Start and finish with potatoes. Cover the dish with a lid or foil. Bake for one hour in a moderate oven (350°F, 180°C or mark 4). Uncover and continue to bake until the top is crisp and golden brown.

Braised Onions — to serve 4-6

800 g small onions
50 g butter
50 g demerara sugar
60 ml stock
Salt and pepper

Peel and blanch the onions. Put the onions in a baking dish. Dot them with the butter. Sprinkle them with the sugar, salt and pepper. Pour the stock around the onions. Cover the dish with a lid or foil. Bake in a moderate oven (350°F, 180°C or mark 4) for about 1½ hours until the onions are tender and golden brown.

Cheese and Onion Dip	To serve 4 for lunch and up to 10 as a party dip

Small bunch of spring onions
200 g cream cheese
Small carton of soured cream
50 g grated cheddar cheese
Salt, pepper, paprika
15 ml thick mayonnaise (optional)
Serving ingredients—A selection from the following: Freshly fried bread fingers, crisps, pieces of cucumber, radishes or raw carrots.

Trim the tops, roots, and outer skins of the onions. Wash them well and chop them very finely. Blend the cream cheese and soured cream. Add the chopped onion, Cheddar cheese, mayonnaise, salt and pepper. Mix well. Put the dip in a small bowl and chill until required. Sprinkle with paprika. Put the bowl in the middle of a large platter and surround it with the serving ingredients.

PARSNIPS

Roast Parsnips	to serve 4

4 medium-sized parsnips

Peel the parsnips. Cut each lengthwise. Boil gently in salted water for 10 minutes. Drain and then dry on kitchen paper and put around a roasting joint of beef or lamb one hour before the meat is cooked, or cook separately with lard. Baste the parsnips when first put into the baking tin.

Sweet Buttered Parsnips	to serve 4

½ kg parsnips
50 g butter
Demerara sugar

Peel and wash the parsnips. Cut into large dice. Steam or boil until tender. Melt butter in a saucepan. Add the parsnips and toss lightly until most of the butter is absorbed. Sprinkle the parsnips with sugar and serve.

Glazed Parsnips	to serve 4

600 g parsnips
50 g brown sugar
35 g butter
juice of ½ lemon
140 ml orange juice or cider
5 ml salt

Wash, boil and peel the parsnips. Drain well and slice them thinly. Butter a shallow baking dish. Arrange half the parsnip slices in a layer in the dish. Mix the salt, sugar, melted butter, lemon and orange juice. Pour half of this over the parsnips. Arrange the rest of the parsnip slices on top and pour the rest of the sugar mixture over them. Bake in a fairly hot oven (400°F, 200°C or mark 6) for about 20 minutes or until the tops of the parsnips are glazed.

Parsnip Chips	to serve 4

½ kg parsnips
25-50 g plain flour
Salt
Deep fat for frying
25 g grated cheese
Parsley for garnishing

Wash and peel the parsnips. Cut as for potato chips. Soak for 30 minutes in cold water to crisp the vegetables. Put into a saucepan. Cover with cold water and add salt. Bring to the boil and cook for 5 minutes or until just tender. Drain thoroughly. Dry. Toss into flour until evenly coated. Heat the fat. Fry the chips for 5 to 8 minutes until golden brown. Drain and turn on to absorbent kitchen paper to absorb excess fat. Serve sprinkled with cheese and garnished with parsley. Parsnip chips are particularly good with lamb chops, bacon, sausages, or chicken.

Other suggestions
1 Dice parsnips. Mix with thickly sliced potatoes and diced bacon or ham. Cook in a covered dish in the oven.
2 Make a purée of parsnips. Add pepper and salt, chopped parsley, a pinch of cinnamon and a little thick cream.
3 Make into soup.

PEAS

Basic Recipe — to serve 4

400-500 g shelled peas
Sprig of mint
5 ml sugar
2.5 ml salt
25 ml butter

If possible pick and shell the peas just before you are going to use them. Put just enough water to cover the peas into a saucepan. Add salt, sugar and mint. Bring the water slowly to the boil. Add peas and simmer until tender but still firm. Drain. Put the peas into a hot vegetable dish. Top with butter.

If frozen peas are used less water will be needed. Follow the instructions on the packet for this and for cooking time. Cook canned peas in the liquid in which they are canned.

Peas and Ham — to serve 4

450 g shelled peas
100 g ham or bacon
50 g butter
10 ml sugar
Pinch of salt
Water or stock

Dice the ham or bacon. Melt half the butter in a saucepan. Add the ham or bacon. Cook gently for 2 to 3 minutes. Add the sugar, salt and peas and just enough water or stock to cover the peas. Bring to the boil. Cover. Lower the heat and cook gently for 25 to 30 minutes. Add the rest of the butter. Serve in the buttery sauce.

Peas Cooked in the French Style — to serve 4

400 g peas
4 spring onions
6 lettuce leaves
2 young carrots
15 ml chopped parsley
50 g butter
60 ml water
10 ml sugar, if needed
Salt and pepper

Tear the lettuce into small pieces. Chop the onions. Cut the carrots into small dice. Put all the ingredients except the sugar into a saucepan. Cover and bring to the boil. Simmer for 20 minutes until the peas are tender and there is about 30 ml of liquid left in the pan. Season to taste and if necessary add the sugar.

Eggs and Peas — to serve 4

400 g peas
5 eggs
70 ml single cream
70 ml water
50 g butter
1 (1.25 ml) spoon each of nutmeg, mace and
    pepper
Sugar and salt

Cook the peas with the spices, butter, water and one (1.25 ml) spoon salt in a shallow casserole, sauté dish or covered frying pan. Taste when they are half cooked and add more salt and sugar if necessary. Make four hollows in the peas with the back of a spoon and break an egg into each hollow. Replace the lid of the pan and simmer for 5 to 10 minutes until the peas are tender and the eggs just set. Beat up the fifth egg with the cream. Pour this over the eggs and peas and grill the dish for a minute or two to set the eggs. Serve immediately from the pan.

Pea Pod Soup — to serve 4

Pods from 1 kg peas
20 g butter
Water or stock
Salt and pepper and sugar
Chopped chives and mint
70 ml single cream (optional)

Simmer pods in salted water or stock with a mint leaf until soft. Sieve or liquidize. Add just enough liquid to make up a litre of thin purée. Return to the pan. Add the butter and sugar. Cook for about ten minutes. Taste to check the seasoning. Serve hot or cold topped with cream, chives and a little mint.

PEPPERS
Some people find the raw skin difficult to digest. If it is grilled or held to a flame until charred black the skin can be rubbed off easily.

Country Omelette	to serve 4

1 red pepper
1 green pepper
100 g bacon
1 medium-sized onion
150 g potatoes
6 eggs
3 tomatoes
A little oil
Salt and pepper
50 g grated cheese (optional)

Peel the tomatoes and chop into small pieces. Cut the potatoes into .5 cm dice. Finely chop the onion. Chop the bacon. Halve the peppers. Remove the seeds, core any white pith. Slice the peppers finely. Pour in enough oil just to coat the bottom of a frying pan. Cook the peppers, bacon, onion and potatoes until cooked and golden brown. Add the tomatoes. Cook gently for a few minutes. Beat the eggs and season them well with salt and pepper. Pour the beaten eggs into the pan. Cook, shaking the pan occasionally to prevent the mixture sticking, until the omelette is golden brown on the underside. If liked, sprinkle the grated cheese over the omelette. Put the pan under a hot grill for a few minutes to set the top of the omelette. Cut the omelette into wedges. Serve with salad.

Pepper Salad	to serve 4

4 medium-sized peppers
4 tomatoes
4 spring onions
Lettuce leaves
15 ml salad oil
15 ml wine vinegar

Salt and black pepper
Parsley

Grill the peppers until the skins blacken, then remove the skins. Cut the peppers in half. Remove the seeds and core. Slice the peppers finely. Skin the tomatoes and then quarter them. Top, tail and remove discoloured skin of the onions then chop them finely. Tear up the lettuce into small pieces. Mix the oil, vinegar, salt and freshly ground black pepper. Mix the peppers, tomatoes and onions. Mix with oil and vinegar dressing. Pile the mixture on to a bed of lettuce. Sprinkle with chopped parsley.

Stuffed Peppers	to serve 4

4 peppers
Salt

Filling: see below

Cut off the top of the peppers and reserve them. Take out the seeds and core. Put the peppers and tops in a pan. Cover them with boiling water. Add salt and cook for five minutes. Drain and cool. Stand them in patty tins or rings on baking sheets. Fill with one of the mixtures suggested below. Replace the tops. Bake in a moderate oven (350° F, 180°C or mark 4) until the filling is cooked.

1 *Cheese filling*
    50 g grated cheese
    1 egg
    150 g cottage cheese
    Freshly ground pepper
    Mix ingredients together

2 *Beef and mushroom filling*
    200 g minced beef
    100 g mushrooms
    2 shallots, chopped
    2 tomatoes, diced
    25 g cornflour
    30 ml oil
    140 ml beef stock
    Pinch of dried thyme
    Salt and pepper

Cook the beef, shallots and mushrooms in the oil. Remove and stir in the tomatoes. Cook slightly. Pour off the excess oil leaving about a tablespoonful. Add the cornflour to the oil. Stir until smooth and cook for one minute. Add the stock, thyme and the beef and mushroom mixture. Season.

3 *Fish filling*
  2 slices white bread
  Milk
  1 beaten egg
  200 g cooked fish
  Salt and pepper
  Pinch dried herbs

Soak bread in milk. Beat together all the filling ingredients.

4 *Vegetable filling*
  100 g onion, finely chopped
  25 g butter
  100 g grated carrot
  100 g mushrooms, sliced
  100 g sweetcorn kernels
  75 g ground nuts
  6 ml dried rosemary, thyme and sage mixed
  10 ml vegetable extract
  Salt and pepper

Melt the butter. Add the herbs and onion and cook slightly. Add the carrots, vegetable extract and cook for two minutes. Add the rest of the ingredients and cook for two or three minutes. Season to taste.

Kebabs   to serve 4

---

2 green peppers
8 small mushrooms
4 tomatoes
4 small onions
6 rashers bacon
400 g lean lamb or pork
Salt and pepper
Oil

Cut the pepper in half. Discard seeds and core. Cut the pepper flesh into 3 cm squares. Quarter the tomatoes. Wipe the mushrooms. Peel the onions. Cut the meat into 3 or 4 cm cubes. Cut the bacon rashers in half. Roll up the half rashers. (You will need 8 skewers, 2 for each person.) Thread the meat and vegetables neatly on to the skewers. Sprinkle with salt and pepper. Put the filled skewers on to a flat dish. Pour a little oil over them. Rotate the skewers and use a brush to make sure all the vegetables and meat pieces are coated with oil. Leave for half an hour. Place the kebabs on a grid in a grill pan under a hot grill. Cook, turning the skewers frequently so that food is evenly cooked. Brush with oil as necessary. Serve on a bed of savoury rice, accompanied by a green salad.

PLANTAINS
Ripe plantains can be peeled as easily as bananas. Green plantains need a different technique because the skin tends to cling tightly to the flesh. Cut off the ends of the plantain, then cut the plantain in half. Take each half, slit through the skin right along the length in four places. Lift the skin away from the flesh along the slits. Remove the fibrous strands clinging to the flesh before cooking as these darken.

Fried Plantain   to serve 4

---

4 plantains
Egg (optional)
Groundnut oil
Salt

Peel the plantains. Slice in diagonal slices. Fry in shallow groundnut oil. They can be served like this or fried, dipped in whipped salted egg and fried again. These can be served with shell fish or with pork.

Curried Plantains   to serve 4

---

6 plantains
40 g butter or margarine
15 ml curry powder
50 g grated coconut
5 ml salt
5 ml pepper
350 ml milk
1 egg

Peel and slice the plantains. Heat the butter. Fry the curry powder for 2 minutes. Add the plantain slices and the coconut and brown lightly. Add the salt, pepper and the milk. Stir well. Simmer over low heat for 30 minutes. Remove from the heat. Stir in the egg. Serve with any rice dish or with plain boiled rice.

Stuffed Plantains Puerta Rican   to serve 4
(Pionanas)

---

2 plantains
25 g butter
Corn oil for frying
Egg
Filling
300 g minced beef
1 green pepper, deseeded and minced
1 onion, chopped
1 tomato, chopped
20 ml oil
Salt and pepper

Blend all the ingredients for the filling. Fry over low heat until cooked, about 20 minutes. Slice each plantain in four, lengthwise. Fry the plantain strips in butter until tender, about 7 minutes. Curve the slices into rings and fix in position with cocktail sticks. Pack the filling into the rings. Brush both sides with egg and fry in hot corn oil for a few minutes.

POTATOES

Basic Recipe—Baked Potatoes

Allow one large potato for each person. King Edwards and Golden Wonder are excellent for baking. New potatoes do not bake well. Choose firm, smooth potatoes, free from blemishes.

Scrub the potatoes with a vegetable brush. Dry them. Prick them deeply all over with a fork. This will help to prevent the skins bursting.

To speed up the cooking time push a skewer or a large clean nail through each potato. The metal conducts the heat into the middle of the potato. You can purchase potato bakers which consist of a series of spikes on which you impale the potatoes.

Put the potatoes on to a baking tin or directly on the oven rack. Bake at any convenient temperature between 350 F and 450 F. In a moderate oven (350°F, 180°C or mark 4) large potatoes take approximately 1 hour 20 minutes. In a hot oven (450°F, 230°C or mark 8) they will take about 45 minutes. To test for readiness pick up

the potato in a cloth. Squeeze the sides. If it feels soft it is cooked. Remove the skewer or nail. Cut a cross into the top of each potato, squeeze the sides so that the steam escapes and the cross opens up. Put a knob of butter in each or leave plain. If the serving dish is left uncovered the potatoes will stay fluffy and dry.

Stuffed Baked Potatoes

Bake the potatoes as above. When you remove the potatoes from the oven halve them lengthwise. With a spoon scoop out the potato flesh without breaking the skins. Mix the potato with the ingredients of one of the fillings suggested below. Mash until smooth and season well. Put the mixture back into the shells. Heat in the oven for a few minutes or brown under the grill.

Fillings
1 For each large potato allow 50 g minced cooked meat or sausage meat, cooked onion, 10 g butter, a little milk, salt and pepper.

2 For each large potato allow 25 to 50 g grated cheese, milk, salt and pepper. If liked, add finely chopped cooked onions or chopped chives.

Irish Potato Cakes   to serve 4

If you are baking potatoes for lunch or supper cook a few extra to make use of the oven heat. Make potato cakes to serve with breakfast the next day.

5 medium-sized baked potatoes
50 g butter
30 ml milk
100 g self-raising flour (extra flour may be needed if an egg is used).
Egg (optional)

Melt the butter in a small saucepan. Remove pan from heat and add the milk. Scoop out the flesh of the potatoes. Mash this until fluffy and quite free of lumps. Add the butter and milk (and the egg). Beat until smooth. Stir in the flour. Knead until smooth on a floured board. Roll out to 1.5 cm thick. Cut into small round cakes. Put on to a greased baking sheet and bake in a moderate oven (350°F, 180°C or mark 4) for 20 minutes, turning the cakes over after 10 minutes to allow them to brown evenly on both sides, or fry on a griddle or in a thick frying pan.

Basic Recipe—Boiled Potatoes

Allow one medium-sized old potato for each person or 450 g of new potatoes for four people.

Old potatoes. Scrub the potatoes. Peel thinly removing eyes and blemishes. Use whole or cut into convenient size. Boil in salted water for 15 to 20 minutes depending on the size of the potatoes. Drain well. Dry over low heat. Toss in melted butter and serve sprinkled with freshly chopped parsley.

New potatoes. Scrub these well. Scrape or leave unpeeled. Cook as for old potatoes (with the addition of mint), rubbing off the skin once the potatoes are cooked.

Some potatoes blacken when peeled and exposed to air, or after cooking. If potatoes must be peeled in advance of cooking cover them in cold salted water to exclude air. Blackening after cooking, which is caused by an acid and iron in the potatoes, can be prevented by adding a few drops of vinegar or lemon juice to the cooking water.

Basic Recipe—Potato Salad   to serve 8

This will keep well in a refrigerator for 48 hours. The flavour improves during this time.

1 kg of new potatoes
60 ml prepared French dressing
15 ml finely chopped onion
15 ml finely chopped parsley
140 ml mayonnaise
5 ml French mustard
15 ml lemon juice
15 ml boiling water

Boil the potatoes in their skins until almost tender. Drain. Return to a low heat covered with a clean tea towel. *Take care: tuck the towel well into the saucepan so that there is no danger of it catching fire.* Cook gently for a further 3 or 4 minutes. The cloth will absorb the steam. The

potatoes will be firm and tender and absolutely dry. Spread the potatoes on to the cloth and leave until cold enough to handle. Skin and slice, or dice into a bowl. Mix the dressing with the onions and parsley and stir these through the potatoes. Blend the mayonnaise, mustard, water and lemon juice. Spoon this mixture on top of the potatoes. Leave in a cool place for at least an hour. Just before serving stir the mayonnaise into the salad.

Mashed Potatoes   to serve 4

4 medium-sized potatoes
About 200 ml hot milk

Boil old potatoes as above. Have the hot milk ready. Reserve some of the cooking water. Crush the potatoes with a potato masher or wooden spoon. Beat until fluffy. Add the hot milk gradually as you beat. Use enough milk so that the potatoes will not be dry but not too soft so that they cannot stand up in peaks. If you need more liquid add the cooking water.

Duchesse Potatoes   to serve 4

200 g freshly boiled potatoes
25 g butter
Salt and pepper
1 egg yolk
15 ml cream or 'top of the milk'
A little beaten egg

Melt the butter in a saucepan. Add the potato and beat well. Mix the egg yolk and cream and add these to the potato. Season to taste. Put into a forcing bag with a 1.5 cm rose pipe. Pipe the potato in large roses or whirls on to a greased baking sheet. Lightly brush with beaten egg. Bake in a fairly hot oven (375°F, 190°C or mark 5) for 20 minutes or until golden brown.

Basic Recipe—Deep Fried Potatoes

Remember that hot fat burns. *Take care.*

To make chips for four people you need about 700 g of fat such as clarified dripping or lard or

¾ litre of oil. The melted fat should be at least 8 cm deep in the deep fryer. Cut peeled potatoes into slices a centimetre thick. Cut these slices into strips one centimetre wide. Cover the chips in cold water. Leave them for at least half an hour before frying them. Drain the potatoes. Dry them thoroughly as water causes the fat to splutter. Spread them on to a clean dry absorbent cloth. Roll them up in this (like jam in a Swiss roll). This completes the drying and prevents air discolouring the potatoes. Unroll the cloth and take out chips as needed leaving the rest in the roll. Heat the fat. The temperature will depend on the fat used. Check that it is hot enough by dropping a chip into the fat. The chip should start to change colour within a few seconds. It it browns too quickly the fat is too hot. If it takes longer the fat is not hot enough. Adjust the heat and check again. When the fat is at the right temperature put a single layer of chips in the frying basket. Do not cook too many at a time as this lowers the temperature of the fat and causes the chips to be soggy. Fry until golden. This will take about 5 minutes. Drain the potatoes. Then turn them on to a baking tin covered with absorbent kitchen paper. Repeat until all are done. Just before serving reheat the fat. Put all the chips back into the basket. Fry them until crisp and brown. Drain on absorbent kitchen paper.

PUMPKIN

Baked Pumpkin	to serve 4-6

1 kg pumpkin
50 g butter
50 g brown sugar
75 g chopped stem-ginger (optional)
Salt and pepper

Peel the pumpkin. Cut into 5 cm dice and arrange in a shallow oven dish. Melt the butter and brown sugar and brush this over the pumpkin. Sprinkle with salt and pepper. If liked, sprinkle with chopped ginger. Bake in a moderate oven (350°F, 180°C or mark 4) for about 50 minutes until tender.

Pumpkin Soup	to serve 4

600 g pumpkin flesh
1 litre stock
Small corm garlic
2 sticks celery
Salt and pepper
25 g cornflour
1 chopped onion, 2 grated carrots (optional)

Chop the pumpkin and wash celery. Crush the garlic. Put the stock, pumpkin, celery and garlic into a saucepan. Cook until the pumpkin dissolves, adding more stock if necessary. Blend the cornflour with a little stock. Add to the soup. Cook until creamy. Add salt and pepper to taste.

American Pumpkin Pie	to serve 6

Shortcrust pastry
200 g plain flour
Small pinch salt
100 g mixed lard and margarine

Filling
200 g cooked drained pumpkin flesh
75 g brown sugar
1 (1.25 ml) spoon nutmeg or ginger
1 (1.25 ml) spoon salt
50 ml milk
2 eggs
100 ml double cream

Make shortcrust pastry. Line a 25 cm flan case or pie dish. Chill the case while you make the filling. Mix the filling ingredients in the order listed. Pour the mixture into the pastry case. Bake in a moderate oven (350°F, 180°C or mark 4) for one hour. Cool.

RADISHES
These are usually eaten raw, in salads, with bread and butter or as appetisers. They make very decorative garnishes. They usually need to be trimmed of leaves and tails but all the very young plant is edible. Young radishes may be cooked by blanching for 5 minutes, then stewed in stock until tender or by cooking in curries.

SALSIFY

Basic Recipe

Allow one root for each person. If very long, cut the roots in half. Wash the roots then cook them in boiling salted water for 30 minutes or until tender. Rinse well, then remove the outer skin. If you wish to peel the roots before cooking you should add a little lemon juice or vinegar to the cooking water to prevent the roots turning black. After being cooked in this way salsify can be treated in a number of ways. It can be used by itself as a vegetable, served with melted butter, or mixed with other ingredients.

Salsify in Butter and Lemon   to serve 4
---

4 roots salsify
5 ml salt
50 g butter
15 ml lemon juice
20 g chopped parsley

Cook the salsify in boiling salted water for 30 minutes. Rinse the roots and remove the skin. Cut the salsify into 10 cm pieces. Melt the butter in a saucepan and cook until nut brown. Add the salsify, lemon juice and parsley and simmer for 10 minutes until the salsify is heated through. Serve with fish or meat or as a course on its own with grated cheese.

Salsify Fritters   to serve 4
---

4 roots salsify
Salt and pepper

Coating batter
50 g flour
Pinch of salt
10 ml salad oil
60 ml water
1 egg white

Garnish
Lemon quarters

Parsley
Grated cheese

Oil for frying

Make the batter. Sieve the flour and salt into a bowl. Make a well in the centre. Add the oil and water. Stir in from the centre gradually drawing in the flour. Beat until smooth. Whisk the egg white until stiff and fold into the mixture with a metal spoon. Peel the cooked roots, cut them into 10 mm slices. Sprinkle them with salt and pepper. Dip the slices in the butter and fry them in hot fat for 5 to 7 minutes until golden brown. Drain and serve hot garnished with lemon, parsley and cheese.

SPINACH

Basic Recipe   to serve 4

600-800 g spinach
Salt and pepper
50 g butter
Nutmeg

Pick off the tough bits of stalk and any damaged parts of the leaves. Wash thoroughly using two or three changes of water. Drain in a colander. Put the spinach in a heavy saucepan. Add salt but no water. Put the lid on the saucepan. Cook over a low heat, tossing occasionally to prevent the leaves sticking to the pan. Cook until tender but avoid overcooking. Drain well. Turn the spinach on to a chopping board and chop it roughly. Just before the spinach is to be served melt the butter in the pan. Return the spinach to the pan and reheat it, stirring the spinach until the butter is absorbed. Season it with salt and a sprinkle of nutmeg. If the spinach is still too moist leave it over low heat for a short time to dry it out.

Eggs Florentine   to serve 4

600-800 g spinach
Salt and pepper
50 g butter
4 eggs
¼ litre cheese sauce
50 g grated Cheddar cheese

36

Cook the spinach in the usual way (see previous recipe). Turn this onto a shallow ovenproof dish. Make four shallow hollows in the spinach with the back of a spoon. Break an egg into each hollow. Pour over the cheese sauce and sprinkle with the grated cheese. Bake in a moderate oven (350 F, 180°C or mark 4) for 40 to 45 minutes until the eggs are set and the top is golden.

Cream of Spinach Soup	to serve 4

400 g spinach
40 g butter
1 litre white stock
Pinch of grated nutmeg
2.5 ml salt
2.5 ml castor sugar
Fried croutons

Wash and cook the spinach in the usual way. Put the cooked spinach, butter, salt and sugar in the pan. Cook for 10 minutes, stirring constantly. Add the stock. Bring the soup to the boil. Rub through a sieve or liquidize. Serve with fried croutons.

SWEDES

Basic Recipe	to serve 4

400-600 g swedes
Salt

Peel the swedes thickly then slice thinly. Cook in boiling salted water for 20 to 30 minutes or until tender. Serve with a white sauce or mashed with butter.

Fluffy Swedes	to serve 4

1 large swede
25 g butter
Salt and pepper
45 ml double cream
15 ml chopped parsley or chives

Peel and roughly chop the swede. Cook until really tender in boiling salted water. Drain well. Mash, sieve or liquidize with butter, salt and pepper. Return to a clean saucepan. Add the cream and beat over low heat with a wire whisk until the mixture is light and fluffy. Pile on to a heated dish. Sprinkle with chopped parsley or chives. Minced ham can be mixed in with the cream. Fluffy swedes are very good with roast beef.

Roast Swede	to serve 4

400-600 g swede
Salt

Peel and cut the swedes into large dice. Parboil them in salt water. Drain well. Roast them under the joint of meat as you would potatoes or in a tin with melted lard or dripping.

SWEETCORN

Roast Corn

Allow one large cob per person. Leave the leaves and silks on the cob. Bake the cobs in a moderate oven (350°F, 180°C or mark 4) for approximately 30 minutes. Remove the leaves and silks. Serve the corn on the cob with plenty of butter.

Boiled Corn on the Cob

Remove the leaves and silks from the cob. Boil the cobs in boiling salted water for 5 to 8 minutes. Avoid overcooking as this toughens the kernels. Drain well. Serve with plenty of butter or with syrup.

Corn off the Cob

Cut or grate the corn from the cob. Melt 10 g of butter for every cob used. Put the corn into the butter. Simmer in a closed pan for a few minutes until the corn is hot and tender. Season with salt and pepper. Add a little cream or top of the milk.

Corn Soup   to serve 4

---

200 g corn kernels (fresh, frozen or canned)
600 g potatoes
1 onion
½ litre stock
1 bay leaf
¼ litre milk
Salt and pepper

Peel and slice the potatoes. Peel and chop the onion. Put the corn, potatoes and onion into the pan with the stock, salt, pepper and bay leaf. Simmer the soup for about half an hour or until the vegetables are tender. Take out the bay leaf. Sieve or liquidize the soup. Add the milk. Reheat, but do not boil the soup.

Scalloped Corn   to serve 4

---

300 g corn kernels (fresh, frozen or canned)
2 eggs
300 ml milk
Salt and pepper
4 small firm tomatoes
4 rashers bacon
½ onion

Chop the onion. Slice the tomatoes. Cut the rind off the bacon. Beat the two eggs with the milk. Add 5 ml salt and a little freshly ground black pepper. Add the corn. Pour the egg and corn mixture into a buttered pie dish. Arrange the tomato slices on top pushing them down into the mixture. Lay the bacon on the top. Cook uncovered in a moderate oven (350°F, 180°C or mark 4) for about 45 minutes or until the mixture is set. A knife stuck in the middle should come out clean.

Corn Fritters   to serve 4-6

---

50 g plain flour
30 ml milk

Pinch of cayenne
Pinch of paprika
1.5 ml salt
1 large egg
150 g cooked sweetcorn kernels
1 egg white
Oil or butter for cooking
Parsley

Whisk the egg white. Beat together the flour, milk, whole egg and seasoning. Add the corn. Fold in the egg white. Drop tablespoons of the mixture into a little hot fat or oil in a frying pan. Turn the fritters as they brown. Serve the fritters hot. Garnish with parsley.

Sweetcorn Flan   to serve 4

Shortcrust pastry
150 g plain flour
75 g mixed lard and margarine
Pinch of salt

Filling
2 eggs
200 g corn kernels
150 ml tomato juice
Salt and pepper
Parsley

Grease a 20 cm flan ring or sandwich tin. Make the shortcrust pastry. Line the flan ring or sandwich tin. If you are using canned corn, drain off the liquid. Mix the corn and tomato juice. Beat the eggs. Add the corn and tomato juice. Season with salt and pepper. Prick the flan base. Pour the mixture into the flan. Bake the flan in a fairly hot oven (375°F, 190°C or mark 5) for twenty minutes. Reduce the heat to 350°F, 180°C or mark 4). Bake for a further half an hour. Garnish with parsley.

SWEET POTATOES
Sweet potatoes can be cooked in all the same ways as the ordinary potato. The skins of sweet potatoes are more delicate than those of ordinary potatoes so it is essential to handle them carefully. Scrub them gently. Cook them in boiling salted water and drain before peeling them. If you have to use cut potatoes wrap them tightly in foil otherwise much of the flavour will leak out into the water.

Candied Sweet Potatoes	to serve 4

400-600 g sweet potatoes
50 g butter
100 g demerara sugar
140 ml orange juice
Good pinch each of salt and cinnamon
1 clove
Orange slices to decorate

Wash and boil the sweet potatoes in salted water until tender. Drain, peel and quarter the potatoes. Mix the sugar, orange juice, butter, salt and cinnamon in a small pan. Add the clove and simmer for 5 minutes. Put the potatoes into a shallow baking dish. Remove the clove and pour the syrup over the potatoes. Bake in a fairly hot oven (375°F, 190°C or mark 5) for about half an hour. Baste occasionally. Decorate with the orange slices. Serve with pork or ham.

Sweet Potatoes and Apples	to serve 4

4 medium-sized sweet potatoes
4 cooking apples
Lemon juice
70 g brown sugar
60 g butter

Cook the sweet potatoes. Peel and cut them into 1 cm slices. Peel the apples. Slice them very thinly. Cook for about three minutes in a little water. Drain and keep the juice. Grease a baking dish. Place in it alternate layers of sweet potatoes and apples. Sprinkle each layer of apples with sugar and lemon juice. Finish with a potato layer. Dot its top layer with the butter. Pour the apple juice made up to 140 ml with water over the apples and potatoes. Bake for about one hour in a moderate oven (350°F, 180°C or mark 4).

Sweet Potato Puffs	

These can be made with left-over boiled or mashed sweet potatoes.

Boil, drain and mash sweet potatoes. Moisten with milk or orange juice. Add salt and butter. Shape into 5 cm balls. Brush with melted butter. Roll in cornflakes, chopped crisp bacon or chopped nuts. Put on to a greased baking sheet. Bake in a moderate oven (350°F, 180°C or mark 4) until pale brown.

TOMATOES

To skin tomatoes. Either rotate on a fork over a low gas flame or dip in boiling water. The skin will split and can be removed with a knife.

To fry tomatoes. Peel and thickly slice the tomatoes. Sprinkle with sugar, salt and pepper. Melt butter in a frying pan. Fry the tomato slices on both sides until brown.

To grill tomatoes. Cut in two around the middle. Make a cross cut in the core of the tomato to allow the heat to penetrate. Sprinkle with sugar, salt and pepper. Top with a little butter. Cook under a grill until cooked and browned.

Tomato Salad	to serve 4

½ kg tomatoes
5 g sugar
Chopped chives
Lettuce leaves
15 ml wine vinegar
30 ml salad oil
Salt and pepper

Suggested additions: hard-boiled eggs, shredded ham, olives, salami.

Slice the tomatoes. Put on to a shallow dish with sugar, salt and pepper. Sprinkle with the oil and vinegar dressing. Add chopped chives. Leave as long as possible, turning the tomatoes over once or twice. Serve in a dish lined with lettuce leaves.

Baked Stuffed Tomatoes	to serve 4

4 large or 8 medium-sized tomatoes
Salt and pepper
Toast or fried bread

Filling: see suggestions below

Wash the tomatoes. Remove the stalks. Cut a thin slice from the end opposite the stalk end and reserve. Scoop out most of the pulp leaving a thin lining of tomato and reserve the pulp. Sprinkle the inside of the tomatoes with salt and pepper. Place tomatoes upside down on a rack to drain while you prepare the filling. Stuff the tomatoes and replace the tops. Bake in a shallow dish for 15 to 20 minutes (375°F, 190°C or mark 5). Serve on a round of fried bread or buttered toast.

Fillings
1 Break a whole egg into each tomato.
2 Chopped cooked meat, herbs and finely chopped onion, bound with milk or egg.
3 Cream cheese beaten up with an egg.
4 A mixture of cooked peppers, aubergines and onions with seasoning.
5 Cooked rice and fish with chopped onion, butter, parsley and grated cheese.
6 Canned fish, hard-boiled eggs and parsley bound with mayonnaise.
7 Left-over curry.
8 Fried bacon, chopped onion, breadcrumbs, parsley bound with egg.
9 Chopped cucumber, cauliflower, parsley, green pepper bound with egg.

Stuffed Tomato Salad

Prepare the tomatoes as for baked stuffed tomatoes. Fill with stuffing which does not need cooking such as salad, vegetables, cheese, hard-boiled egg, cooked fish or meat. These can be moistened with mayonnaise. Garnish with small sprigs of parsley. Arrange the stuffed tomatoes on a platter of shredded lettuce, cucumber slices, watercress.

Neapolitan Tomato Sauce	to serve 4

To serve with spaghetti

1 onion
2 small cloves garlic
½ kg tomatoes
Salt and freshly ground pepper
1 (2.5 ml) spoon chopped parsley

1 (2.5 ml) spoon oregano
3 ml olive oil
200-300 g spaghetti, freshly cooked

Peel, slice and finely chop the onion. Crush the garlic. Cook the onion and garlic in the oil until transparent. Peel the tomatoes and chop them coarsely. Add to the onion and garlic with the seasoning and cook over medium heat for five minutes or until fairly thick. Stir in the parsley and oregano. Pour over the freshly cooked spaghetti.

Tomato and Pepper Casserole	to serve 4

2 Spanish onions
90 ml oil
6 ripe tomatoes
1 green pepper
1 red pepper
Small tin tomato concentrate
1 clove garlic
Salt and pepper
Pinch of cayenne pepper
Pinch of paprika
4 eggs
Pinch of powdered cumin

Slice the onions and the tomatoes. Chop the peppers and crush the garlic. Cook the onions in half the oil until they are golden. Add the tomatoes and peppers, tomato concentrate and crushed garlic. Simmer gently until cooked through and soft. Add the rest of the oil, salt and peppper, paprika, cayenne, and simmer for another 5 minutes. Spoon the vegetables into individual casseroles. Break one egg into each and bake in a moderate oven (375°F, 190°C or mark 5) until the eggs are just set. Sprinkle with a pinch of cumin before serving.

Cream of Tomato Soup	to serve 4-6

¾ kg tomatoes
½ onion
1 stick celery
1 clove garlic
1 ml ground mace
1 ml pepper

2.5 ml bicarbonate of soda
25 g butter
50 g flour
1 litre milk
Paprika

Chop the tomatoes, onion, celery and garlic. Put them in a saucepan with the mace and pepper. Cook for 5 minutes. Knead the butter and flour into a ball. Warm the milk. Add the butter and flour ball. Stir until the sauce is smooth and slightly thick. Sieve the tomato mixture. Reheat and add the soda. Stir. Then gradually stir in the white sauce. Warm, but do not allow the soup to boil. Serve hot or cold sprinkled with paprika.

TURNIPS

Basic Recipe	to serve 4

4 young turnips

Peel, slice thinly and boil in salted water for 20 to 30 minutes or until tender. Drain and toss in butter and black pepper or coat with white sauce.

Young turnips do not need to be peeled. They can be cooked first and then the skin can be rubbed off.

Turnip Salad—Uncooked	to serve 4

4 young turnips
Salt
French dressing
Chopped parsley

Peel the turnips and grate them finely. Put them in a bowl and sprinkle with salt. Leave for one hour. Drain off the liquid. Mix with French dressing and sprinkle with chopped parsley.

Roast Turnips	to serve 4

4 young turnips
50 g butter or margarine

50 g flour
Salt and pepper

Peel and slice the turnips. Parboil in salted water for 5 minutes. Drain. Roll in seasoned flour. Melt the butter or margarine in a baking tin. Coat both sides of the turnip with butter. Spread the slices in the tin. Bake in a moderate oven (350°F, 180°C or mark 4) for 30 minutes. If you wish, you could add about 25 g of honey to the butter or scatter the turnips in the tin with curry powder or dried ginger.

Stuffed Turnip Cups	to serve 4

4 medium-sized turnips
Salt, large pinch
140 ml milk

Filling
10 g butter or margarine
15 ml chopped onions
30-40 ml cooked peas
Salt and pepper
Breadcrumbs

Peel then blanch the turnips in salted water for 5 minutes. Hollow into halves, reserving and chopping the pulp. Melt the butter. Cook the onions in this for 2 or 3 minutes. Add the peas and pulped turnip. Season with salt and pepper. Thicken the mixture with breadcrumbs. Fill the turnip cups with the mixture. Put the turnips in a greased baking dish. Combine the milk and salt and pour this around the turnips. Bake until tender, about 20 minutes in a moderate oven (375°F, 190°C or mark 5).

Further suggestions
1 Parboiled turnip slices dipped in batter for frying.
2 Parboiled turnip slices and tomatoes to be baked in butter with a little juice and basil.
3 Use as the basis for a spring soup.
4 Roast turnip slices around duck or pork. They absorb fat from the meat and become tasty and tender.
5 Mix grated turnips, spring onions and cabbage, and fry in cakes or bake in a pie-dish.
6 Glaze in the same way as for parsnips.

WATERCRESS

Sandwich Filling and Spreads

1 Cream cheese, watercress leaves finely chopped, and slices of hard-boiled eggs.
2 Grated carrot, sliced bananas and watercress.
3 Blend chopped watercress leaves with cream cheese.
4 Blend 200 g cottage cheese, 50 g minced cooked chicken and the leaves from a bunch of watercress.
5 Watercress and bananas.
6 Watercress, apple and bacon.

Watercress Soup   to serve 4-6

2-3 bunches watercress
1 onion
1 stick celery
¼ litre milk
25 g butter
¾ litre stock (pale coloured)
Pepper
Pinch of nutmeg

Wash the watercress and remove the stalks. Chop the onion and celery. Put the watercress, onion and celery in a saucepan with just enough water to prevent them burning. Cook until tender. Sieve or liquidize. Return to the saucepan with the milk, butter and stock. Stir it until it boils, season and add nutmeg. Serve with croutons.

Lemon and Watercress Soup   to serve 4

½ litre chicken stock
45 ml lemon juice
½ bunch watercress
2 potatoes
Salt and pepper

Peel the potatoes and grate them. Chop the watercress. Simmer the stock and lemon juice for a few minutes. Add the watercress and potato. Cook for 10 minutes. Season and serve.

Watercress Sauce   to serve 4

1 bunch watercress
A few sprigs parsley
200 ml prepared mayonnaise
30 mm cucumber
Squeeze of lemon
Salt and pepper

Pick the watercress leaves from the stems. Wash them with the parsley and cook both in very little water for 3 minutes. Drain thoroughly. Chop the watercress and parsley and the cucumber. Mix these with the mayonnaise. Add salt and pepper and lemon juice to taste. Chill.

Watercress Salads

1 Watercress with orange sections and finely sliced onions served with a curry dressing.
2 Watercress with sliced mushrooms, diced tomatoes and vinaigrette dressing.
3 Watercress with mixed cooked vegetables.
4 Watercress, fish and shellfish.
5 As one of the ingredients of a green salad.

Other suggestions

1 Simmer watercress in butter and serve with grilled meat.
2 Add chopped watercress to omelettes.
3 Add to stuffing for chicken.
4 Use as a garnish.

YAMS

Baked Yams   to serve 4-6

1 large yam
25 g flour
Pinch of salt
50 g butter
3 (5 ml) spoons milk
Salt and pepper

Peel the yam. Cut it into thick slices. Roll them in salted flour to coat them evenly. Put on to a baking sheet. Bake in a moderately hot oven (375°F, 190°C or mark 4). When the yams are cool enough to handle, cut a thin slice off each piece. Scoop out the soft inner flesh. Mix this with the butter and milk. Season with salt and pepper to taste. Refill the hard skins with the mixture. Brush with a little melted butter. Bake for a further 20 minutes or until golden brown. Serve with fried bacon.

Egg and Yam Fritters

1 thick slice of yam
1 red pepper
1 tomato
¼ onion
Salt
1 egg
Deep fat or oil for frying

Grate the yam. Chop the pepper, tomato and onion. Add salt to taste. Beat the egg and add to the vegetables. Mix well and form into small balls. Fry in hot fat. Drain well and serve hot. Potatoes can be substituted for yams.

Yam chips

Cut peeled yams into chips 1 cm thick and 10 cm long. Fry in hot fat or oil. Serve with fried fish.

Yam Crisps

Slice peeled yams and cut each slice into very thin slices with a slicer, a very sharp knife or a potato peeler. Soak in salted water. Drain and dry. Fry in hot oil for a minute.

Carrot

Bundles. Cut carrots in shoestring sticks. Chill in ice water. Draw several sticks through a carrot ring (see below).

Curls. Cut long, paper-thin strips of carrot using a very sharp knife or a potato peeler. Roll each strip around your finger and fasten with a toothpick. Chill in ice water. Remove toothpicks.

Rings. Cut a medium-size carrot into slices and remove centres. Use for making 'bundles'.

Cauliflower

Flowerets. Break large flowerets into small ones. Chill in ice water. Dry well. Sprinkle with paprika or leave plain.

Celery

Bundles. Cut 7 cm matchstick-thick pieces. Draw several of them through a carrot ring. Chill in iced water. Slightly thicker sticks can be slit at both ends.

Hearts. Use the stalks in the heart of the celery head.

Cucumber

Fingers. Cut peeled or unpeeled cucumber in half lengthwise. If the seeds are large, remove these. Cut solid parts into narrow strips 7 cm long.

Fluted. Score the whole surface of an unpeeled cucumber by running the prongs of a fork lengthwise down the cucumber gouging out the strips of skin. Cut the cucumber in thin crosswise or diagonal slices.

Twists. Cut thin slices of cucumber. Cut from the centre of each slice to the outer edge. Twist the ends in opposite directions.

Cones. Cut wafer-thin slices. Cut from the centre to the outer edge of each slice. Wrap the slice around on itself to make a cone. If the slices are thin enough they will stick together easily if pressed between thumb and finger.

Peppers

Rings. Cut the pepper in thin crosswise slices. Trim away seeds and membrane.

Mock holly. Cut green peppers in pieces the shape of holly leaves. Arrange 2 or 3 leaves with berry-shaped pieces of red pepper.

Radishes

Accordions. Use long radishes with the leaves removed. Cut radishes in thin crosswise slices about three quarters of the way through. Chill in iced water to open them out.

Fans. Use long radish. Cut in thin slices from the root top almost to the leaf end. Spread out to form a fan. Chill in cold water.

Daisies. Make four or five petals by cutting the red peel from the root tip almost down to the stem. Leave a strip of red between each 'petal'. Chill and open the petals in iced water.

Roses. Cut down the centre from the tip almost to the leaf with a sharp knife five or six times. Leave in iced water to open.

Onions

Rings. Peel large mild onions. Cut in thin crosswise slices. Loosen slices into individual rings.

Spring Onions

Bundles. Trim green onions to 10 to 12 cm long. Wrap a carrot curl around two onions or draw the onions through carrot rings.

Flowers. Cut spring onions to 4 to 5 cm lengths using the firm part only. With a sharp knife cut one third of the way down both ends several times. Leave in iced water for several hours or overnight to form flowers.

Tomatoes

Roses. Using a small sharp knife make short zig-zag cuts around the sides of the tomato making sure to cut through the centre core. Pull halves apart gently.

HORS D'OEUVRES

1 Avocado pear halves with a vinaigrette dressing or with a variety of fillings.
2 Raw, sliced, dressed mushrooms.
3 Paper-thin slices of artichoke hearts latticed with anchovies.
4 Tomato slices, dressed with oil and lemon, sprinkled with herbs.
5 Very thinly sliced red peppers dressed with oil and sprinkled with chopped black olives.
6 Russian or potato salads.
7 Cucumber in sour cream sprinkled with freshly milled black pepper.
8 Lettuce, sliced tomato, thin carrot sticks and green pepper rings.
9 Sliced cucumber topped with artichoke hearts.
10 Chicory leaves filled with a variety of savouries such as shellfish, cheese, chopped vegetables.

DRESSINGS AND SAUCES

French Dressing

90 ml olive or salad oil
30 ml good quality vinegar, preferably wine vinegar
1 (1.25 ml) spoon each of salt, pepper and dry mustard
1 (2.5 ml) spoon sugar

Combine all ingredients in a screw-top jar. Shake until these are well blended.

Variations
1 *Garlic dressing.* Add a clove of garlic crushed with a little salt.
2 *Lemon dressing.* Substitute lemon juice for vinegar and add a little grated lemon rind.
3 *Mint dressing.* Add 5 ml finely chopped mint and 5 ml sugar.

Mayonnaise

2 egg yolks
1 (5 ml) spoon castor sugar
1 (2.5 ml) spoon salt, pepper and dry mustard
30 ml wine vinegar
250 ml olive or salad oil in a jug

Put the egg yolks, sugar, salt, pepper and mustard in a bowl. Mix. Gradually add the vinegar. Add the oil literally a drop at a time whisking all the time. Once a third of the oil has been added, the rest of the oil can be added at an increased rate whisking all the time. If the mayonnaise is to be stored add 30 ml boiling water. Store in a cool place, but not a refrigerator at a very cold setting.

Melted Butter Sauce

45 ml water
100 g butter

Bring the water to the boil in a small saucepan. Stir in the butter until completely melted. Remove immediately from the heat. Whisk the sauce until smooth and creamy.

Hollandaise Sauce

30 ml wine vinegar
Large pinch pepper
1 (1.25 ml) spoon salt
10 ml cold water
2 egg yolks
75-100 g butter

Put the vinegar and pepper in the top of a double boiler or in a bowl over a saucepan of boiling water. Heat and reduce the vinegar to about three-quarters. Remove from the heat. Cool. Add the salt, cold water, egg yolks and a little of the butter. Replace over the hot water. Do not boil. Whisk with a wire whisk until the sauce thickens, then whisk in the rest of the butter a little piece at a time until the sauce is as thick as needed. If the sauce starts to curdle add a little more cold water and whisk it in.

White Sauce (Roux method)

25 g butter or margarine
25 g flour
¼ litre of milk for coating consistency, *or* ⅛ litre of milk for a panada or binding sauce, *or* ½ litre for a thin sauce for soups
Seasoning

Heat the butter gently. Remove from the heat. Stir in the flour and seasoning. Heat gently to cook but not brown the flour. Remove from the heat. Blend in the cold milk gradually. Bring to the boil. Cook, stirring all the time with a wooden spoon until the mixture is smooth and of the required consistency.

White Sauce (quick method)

Mix the flour and seasoning in a bowl. Add a quarter of the milk and blend to a smooth paste. Warm the rest of the milk in a saucepan. Pour the hot milk over the flour mixture stirring all the time. Pour the sauce back in the pan. Continue cooking for 5 minutes. Add the butter. Beat the sauce with a wooden spoon or whisk with a wire whisk. Taste and re-season if necessary.

Cheese Sauce

Allow 75-150 g grated cheese and a little mustard to add to the white sauce.

Part 2

Vegetables in the diet

There are at least three hundred thousand different kinds of plants growing in the world. A large number of these are potentially edible but comparatively few have ever been regarded as acceptable for human consumption. Most people are very conservative in their choice of food. Even in times of famine there is a reluctance to eat unfamiliar foods, even those known to be safe.

There are many religious and cultural taboos concerning food, but the vegetables we eat are generally free from these associations. Aversion to strange food is probably the result of sensible precautions taken against accidental poisoning. Our early ancestors, depending on wild plants for survival, had to learn by trial and error which were safe to eat. If someone became ill or died after eating an unfamiliar leaf or root this would be a frightening lesson for the onlookers. All parts of that plant and any of the same appearance would be strictly shunned.

Unfortunately this caution has carried over into our scientific era. There are many plants as yet uncultivated which could be used to help solve the world food problem. If scientists could persuade people that these plants are nourishing, good to eat and safe, it would still take a lot of propaganda before they were accepted as basic foods. Think how often you have heard people

reject certain foods before tasting them. Even young people eager to welcome new ideas and fashions are often reluctant to try unfamiliar foods.

Most of the vegetables we eat originated in the Near East or in the northern regions of South America. There were highly organized societies in both these areas very early in history, and the selection and cultivation of different varieties of vegetables was important to survival. The choice of plants came about over many centuries, and was influenced by a number of factors apart from the elimination of those plants proved to be dangerous or inedible. Here are some of the possible influences, and perhaps you can think of others:

1 Some plants were more readily available than others—depending on climate and soil, ease of cultivation and the materials available for making tools.
2 The flavour, texture and appearance of some plants are more pleasing than others.
3 Plants which can be stored for use in times of food shortage—such as winter, crop failure or siege— are especially valuable and would have been carefully cultivated before canning and deep-freezing were available for food preservation.

The vegetables of today are the descendants of plants which fulfilled these conditions. When introduced into this country many of them, even in recent times, were at first rejected. Food introduced by invaders or refugees usually went out of fashion if the visitors left the country. The Romans brought many continental plants with them and grew them successfully in this country for centuries. When the Romans left, the British reverted to their traditional diet of grains and meat with just a few vegetables.

Not until the Middle Ages was there any real change in this attitude. Then men started to travel more, trading as well as fighting in foreign lands, eating new foods and learning new methods of cultivation.

Until recently we only grew in Britain the plants which would adapt readily to conditions in this country. In spite of this, until the end of the eighteenth century Britain produced all her own food and was regarded as the granary for Europe.

We are fortunate in this country. We are able to grow some of the best vegetables in the world. The soil and climate are suitable for a wide variety of crops. Although this is a small country there are areas of nearly every type of soil. We have adequate supplies of water and if flooding occurs occasionally it is confined to small areas for very short periods. There are few places where really low temperatures are a problem and there are few heatwaves. Insects and weeds which could affect food production can easily be kept under control.

In recent years the patterns of food production and consumption have changed. More children survive and adults live longer than in the past. The standard of living has improved and people expect a wider variety and greater quantity of food than their ancestors had. While there is still widespread hunger and starvation in many parts of the world, it is over-eating and obesity that causes concern in most Western countries.

We are no longer self-supporting. At least half our food comes from overseas. We cannot expect this state of affairs to continue. It is morally wrong that we should expect the underdeveloped countries to supply us with food we could grow for ourselves while their own people are undernourished.

Most vegetables can be grown in this country but we cannot grow sufficient grain to feed our present stocks of farm animals. If people could be persuaded to increase the production and consumption of vegetables and to cut down on the large quantities of animal products now eaten, there could be a significant saving on the money spent on food by the housewife and by the country as a whole.

We are a nation of keen gardeners. It is just as easy to grow vegetables as flowers. There is an overwhelming choice of tools designed to lighten the work. Research stations, plant geneticists, biochemists and makers of herbicides and pesticides are all working to back up the amateur as well as the professional grower.

During the Second World War Britain could not afford the money or the ships to import huge quantities of food. Food was rationed or in very short supply. Most families lucky enough to have a garden or allotment gave priority to food production. They grew large quantities of fruit and vegetables to supplement and add variety to the basic rations. The diet was meagre but sufficient. Most people were healthier and had less dental decay than people today. There was less food but more care was taken in its preparation and little was wasted. While no one would wish to return to the conditions of that time we could put to use many of the lessons in food management learned then.

We will have to find new means of producing more food for ourselves. This involves making better use of the land available (taking into account the rising demand for land for housing, factories and motorways), using improved strains of plants, and learning how to control weeds and insects.

Self-sufficiency and the cutting of waste could go a long way in solving our food problems. The abundance of food available to us has made us careless. A quarter of all the food in this country is wasted. The housewife is not the chief culprit. Farmers, workers in the food industry, shops and restaurants are all guilty. Food which could be eaten is discarded too readily. A good deal of food unsuitable for human consumption could be used as animal food and fertilizer, or even recycled for human food. The cost of wastage is reflected in the higher cost of food actually consumed.

In the past twenty years agriculturalists in this country have doubled the output of food and it is

49

estimated that even this can be improved. It would be a pity if all this effort should be wasted by lack of interest or carelessness and we were to bring about a shortage of food in Britain.

VALUE OF VEGETABLES IN THE DIET
Vegetables are an inexpensive source of some vitamins and mineral salts. They also contain varying quantities of carbohydrates. A few are a minor source of protein. They are all poor in fat.

Carbohydrates
These are a source of heat and energy. There are several classes of carbohydrates and different vegetables contain different carbohydrates:
1 Starch—mainly in potatoes
2 Sugar—in beetroot, cabbage, carrots, leeks, sweetcorn, tomatoes, onions
3 Starch and sugar mixture—in broad beans, parsnips, peas
4 Cellulose—this makes up the cell walls; it cannot be digested by human beings but is used as roughage.

Protein
Protein foods are needed for growth and repair of the body. Proteins are made up of twenty-two amino-acids. Not all are present in every protein food. Ten of the amino-acids are essential but cannot be made by the body. Animal proteins contain all these ten amino-acids in the correct proportions. With the exception of soya beans, vegetable proteins do not contain all the essential ten amino-acids. Pulse foods are the main source of vegetable protein. There are negligible quantities in most other vegetables.

Vitamin A
This can be stored by the body to be used when needed. It is fat soluble. It is necessary for growth in children and is sometimes known as the anti-infective vitamin. It protects the skin and helps to keep the lining of the throat, lungs and stomach healthy. It helps the eyesight, particularly for seeing in dim light.

Vegetables are not a direct source of Vitamin A. The green and yellow colouring in fruit and vegetables contains carotene which can be converted into Vitamin A by the body during digestion. If vegetables and fruit are the sole source of Vitamin A, very large quantities are needed as it takes three parts of carotene to convert one part Vitamin A. The main sources of carotene are broccoli, the outer leaves of cabbage, carrots, kale, spinach, tomatoes, turnip tops and watercress.

Vitamin B Thiamine
This is important for the maintenance of a strong nervous system and in helping release energy from carbohydrate foods. It helps in growth and is essential for a good skin and for muscular control. Thiamine is water soluble. It is present in most vegetables but especially peas, beans, and green vegetables.

Vitamin B Riboflavin
This is necessary for the steady growth of children. It keeps the mouth and tongue free from infection and keeps the cornea of the eyes clear. There is unlikely to be a shortage of this vitamin in a sensible mixed diet. Riboflavin is water soluble. It is available in broccoli, lettuce and spinach.

Vitamin C
This is the vitamin most likely to be lacking in the diet. It is very easily lost from food during storage and cooking. It is water soluble so daily supplies are needed. It is destroyed by heat. Vitamin C helps the body to resist infection, keeps the skin and gums healthy, and is important in the healing of wounds and fractures. It helps in growth. It is available in varying quantities in a wide range of vegetables:
Very high content—in broccoli, kale, peppers, turnip tops
High—in cabbage, cauliflower, spinach, watercress
Moderate—in broad beans, leeks, spring onions, new potatoes, radishes, swedes
Low—in lettuce, tomatoes.

Calcium
This is needed in the formation and hardening of teeth and bones, for the clotting of the blood and to enable muscles to function properly. It is present in most vegetables but especially celery, kale, watercress and root vegetables.

Iron
Iron is needed for the formation of haemoglobin of the red corpuscles of the blood. Small quantities are present in most vegetables but especially in broad beans, endive, peas and watercress. Though present in spinach it is rendered useless by the oxalic acid in the plant.

Water
All vegetables contain a high percentage of water.

This makes them very bulky foods, excellent as part of a slimming diet.

CLASSIFYING VEGETABLES

Vegetables may be classified in several ways, and when planning meals you should consider them from several aspects.

Part of plant

Different parts of plants provide different nutrients, colour and texture. It is sensible to serve vegetables that come from different parts of plants rather than several roots or several different seeds. The exception to this rule is salads.

Part of the plant	Example
Roots	beetroot, carrots, parsnips, radishes
Tubers	potato, Jerusalem artichoke
Bulbs	onions
Stems	asparagus, celery
Leaves	cabbage, lettuce, spinach, watercress
Flowers	artichoke, broccoli, cauliflower
Seeds	beans, peas, sweetcorn
Fruit	aubergine, cucumber, marrow, tomato

Some vegetables do not fit exactly into these categories. The entire plant of the mushroom and truffle is eaten. More than one part of a number of vegetables is edible.

Colour

Colour plays an important part in meal planning. Harmonizing colours add interest and variety to the most simple meal. One-colour meals are flat and monotonous.

Colour	Example
Green	leaf vegetables, sprouts, peas, broccoli, peppers
Yellow	carrots, sweetcorn, sweet potato, peppers
White	cauliflower, turnips, onions, parsnips
Red	beetroot, radish, red cabbage, tomatoes, peppers

Flavour

Flavours should be balanced. As a general rule only one strongly flavoured vegetable should be served in a meal.

Flavour	Example
Mild	mushrooms, sweetcorn, peas, beans
Strong	onions, broccoli, turnips

Texture

It is important to provide contrasting textures.

Texture	Example
Crisp	lettuce, raw carrot, celery, radish
Soft	tomato, marrow, aubergine, mushroom

Buying and Storing

SHOPPING FOR VEGETABLES

Fruit and vegetables must be used quickly if you are to get the full food value. They deteriorate very quickly even under quite good standards of storage. It is very easy to be tempted by an attractive display and to purchase vegetables which you do not really need. There are a number of places where you can purchase vegetables. Each has advantages and disadvantages.

Nursery and farm shops and stalls

Produce bought directly from the grower is the most likely to be freshly picked or dug and the prices may sometimes be a little lower than the retail price. There may be a cool shady building or stall to display the stock. Vegetables left out in sunlight at the roadside on a hot day will quickly deteriorate. It is not economical to make long journeys just to buy vegetables, but you may see goods you wish to purchase when on a day out. Do not make any purchases at the beginning of the day. A hot car is a poor place to keep fresh vegetables. Keep a few carrier bags in the car as there is often a shortage of packaging in these shops.

In some places the Women's Institute run produce stalls where people with gardens or allotments bring their surplus for sale. Goods are often of excellent value.

Wholesale markets

Goods are sold at wholesale prices so this is an economical way to purchase goods for stocking up the deep-freezer or to shop for several families. You nearly always have to buy in bulk, although occasionally some wholesalers will sell smaller quantities at the end of a session when they have dealt with all their usual customers. You will have to carry your own purchases so a shopping trolley is essential, and if you are getting several vegetables you will need private transport.

Supermarkets

You can spend as much time as you like deciding what to buy. There is usually a good range of vegetables including some varieties not always to be seen in small shops. The large turnover usually means that goods are fresh and offered at competitive prices. If pre-packed goods are sold, scales should be available for you to check the weights. If the shop is one of a chain, the buyer of fruit and vegetables will be an experienced specialist trained to purchase the best quality goods at competitive prices. You will benefit from his expertise. Supermarkets usually carry a wide range of frozen, canned and dried vegetables. One drawback is that the supermarkets are often very warm, not the ideal atmosphere for vegetables. Customers often handle goods carelessly so be wary of bruised vegetables and make quite sure you wash all unwrapped goods extra carefully.

Small retail shops
The service here will depend on the knowledge and interest of the manager, often the owner.

If he is efficient he will know his customers' requirements, do his own buying at wholesale markets and be prepared to deal with special orders. Find out which days he gets in fresh supplies. Some shops make up orders for delivery or collection but it is sensible to shop in person unless you have complete confidence in your greengrocer. Many retail shops sell frozen, canned and dried vegetables.

Market stalls
These will vary. In established markets traders rent stalls. They are registered with the local authority and display their names and addresses, thus giving as much assurance or reliability as the small shop. It is not profitable for traders to hold over large stocks of vegetables from one market to another so prices tend to go down towards the end of the day. The casual unregistered stall-holder or barrow-boy might not be so reliable. A display of prime goods on the front of the stall might hide inferior products at the back to be sold to the unwary shopper. No redress is available from the casual stall-holder if the goods are not up to the expected standard.

Mobile shops
In some areas salesmen with mobile shops make regular deliveries of fruit and vegetables. As a rule, because of the size of the shop there is not a wide choice. In some cases only potatoes are sold but as the quantity needed for a family could be heavy to carry from ordinary shops it could be worth while using this service. Deliveries are seldom made more than once a week so they may only be useful as an additional shopping facility.

CHOOSING VEGETABLES
Vegetables in season are usually at their lowest price and highest food value. They should be eaten as soon as possible after being picked, cut or dug out of the ground, as after this the vegetable starts to deteriorate. Deterioration of nutrition, taste and texture varies according to the plant. For this reason it is worth while growing your own vegetables so that you can consume them at their very best. Purchase frequently the quantity you can use within a very short time.

Green vegetables
Look for plants with fresh crisp leaves of a good colour. If leaves are limp or yellow or the stem is shrivelled, the plant should be rejected. Lettuces and cabbages should have firm hearts. Plants should be heavy for their size. Greengrocers sometimes strip off outer leaves of green vegetables which have been in the shop too long. Look out for this and reject such plants. The dark outer leaves have the highest food value. Even if the rest of the plant appears fresh it will be past its prime. Do not purchase half a cabbage even if it is offered at a low cost, as the loss of vitamins from the cut surface will be high.

Root vegetables
These should have unblemished skins free from spongy or discoloured patches. They should be small to medium but heavy for their size. Very large vegetables can be coarse textured and of poor flavour. Avoid any with an excessive amount of soil clinging to them but remember that washed vegetables will deteriorate more quickly than those left unwashed.

Other vegetables such as pods, stems and fruits
Pods should be full but not overcrowded. They should be of good colour without brown marking or any appearance of drying out. Look at the shopping notes for each vegetable in Chapter 6. As a general rule choose vegetables which are really fresh and of good colour and texture.

CARE OF VEGETABLES IN THE HOME
Strictly speaking vegetables should not be stored in the home but purchased in small quantities and used immediately. However, this advice would be of little help to an elderly person or a mother of several small children living a long distance from the greengrocer. Several trips to the greengrocers each week would be impractical. However, vegetables should be eaten daily. It is important that they should be stored so that they will keep in the best possible condition with the minimum of wastage and the maximum food value.

Root vegetables and tubers
Root vegetables need cool airy storage. A wire vegetable rack fulfils this function. The large, flat box-type racks are preferred to the round basket kind, as the vegetables can be spread out and air

can circulate around them. A stuffy closed cupboard is not suitable. Neither should the vegetables be in full sunlight.

Potatoes need special care. They should be kept in the dark even if this merely means keeping them in a thick, brown paper bag. The light causes them to turn green. This green colouring contains the toxic solanine which makes the potatoes bitter and unfit for use. The storage temperature should be at 5° to 10°C to prevent the starch being converted into sugar and to inhibit sprouting. Turnips and parsnips need slightly moist storage to keep them in good condition.

Large quantities of root vegetables, usually the produce of the garden or allotment, should be stored in bulk in clamps in the open. Long heaps are put into shallow trenches lined with straw. They are then covered with straw, then with earth to exclude air. Smaller quantities may be covered with dry soil or ashes in a cool shed. Some vegetables improve by being left in the ground until, after several frosts, they may be dug up as needed.

Green leaf vegetables
Green leaf vegetables should not be kept for more than a day or two after purchase as the loss of water leads to wilting and loss of Vitamin C. Wash and dry the leaves carefully and quickly. Wrap in foil or an airtight plastic bag. Store in the vegetable drawer of a refrigerator until you are ready to cook them. If you do not have the use of a refrigerator, put the wrapped vegetables in a tightly-lidded plastic or tin box or saucepan. Put this in a cool place.

Canned, frozen and dried vegetables
Canned vegetables should be stored in a cool, dry place. They will keep for many months but it is best to use one season's supply before the next year's crop comes on the market. Even under perfect conditions there is a gradual loss of quality and nutritive value with prolonged storage. As soon as the can is opened deterioration takes place as quickly as for cooked fresh vegetables.

Frozen vegetables should be put immediately into the freezing compartment of a refrigerator or in a freezer and left there until it is time to cook them. Commercially frozen food-packs are marked with stars to indicate the length of time you can safely store them in a larder, a refrigerator or a freezer. Frozen vegetables will keep for months if they are not allowed to defrost. If vegetables do thaw out they should be cooked immediately since, if left in a thawed and uncooked state, they will soon spoil.

Dried vegetables keep well if stored in tightly-covered containers in a cool, dry place.

Checking stored vegetables
Stored vegetables should be checked frequently, fresh vegetables every day. Discard decayed vegetables immediately as they will quickly spoil those around them. Try to use up vegetables before deterioration sets in. Any which are limp but edible can be used up in soups or curries. While they may have lost a lot of Vitamin C they are still valuable for their mineral content and as roughage. For storage notes on each vegetable, see Chapter 6.

Cooking

For basic preparation of individual vegetables see the recipe section. When cooking vegetables you should aim to retain as much nutritive value as possible. The cooked vegetables should be pleasing in colour, flavour and texture. When fresh vegetables are cooked the cellulose framework is softened and the starch and protein released and cooked. Thiamine, Vitamin C and some minerals dissolve readily in water and these vitamins can be destroyed by heat. To prevent the loss of nutrients these rules should be followed:

1 Use vegetables as soon as possible after picking. Store for the minimum time under the best conditions.
2 Avoid bruising the vegetables. Use a really sharp knife when cutting vegetables. A blunt knife bruises the tissues.
3 Whenever possible serve the vegetables raw.
4 Wash as necessary but do not soak for any longer than necessary to remove dirt.
5 Shred green vegetables. Cut up other vegetables in small pieces. This will cut down the time needed for cooking.
6 Cook in a pan with a tightly fitting lid. Use as little boiling water as possible. Keep the cooking time to the minimum.
7 Drain the vegetables and serve immediately. Foods kept hot or reheated lose most of their vitamin content.

8 The cooking water will contain dissolved vitamins and mineral salts. Save this and use it as soon as possible for soup, gravy or sauces.

RETAINING COLOUR
During cooking, green vegetables sometimes become a slightly brownish colour because of changes which take place in the chlorophyll. This is less likely to occur if the vegetables are cooked very quickly. White vegetables, such as cauliflower and onion, may become yellowish in colour and red vegetables such as red cabbage and beetroot turn slightly purplish. A small amount of vinegar or lemon juice added to the cooking water will help prevent colour changes.

RETAINING FLAVOUR
The freshness of the vegetables will make a considerable difference to their flavour when cooked. As vegetables (with the exception of potatoes) age, some of the sugar turns to starch. Some of the compounds which give vegetables their individual flavours are volatile and escape with the steam when they are boiled. This can be lessened if the minimum of water is used and the vegetables cooked in a tightly lidded pan. Prolonged cooking of vegetables of the cabbage family develops strong unpleasant flavours.

TEXTURE OF VEGETABLES
Most vegetables have a pleasant crisp texture if cooked for the correct time. If crispness is distasteful a softer texture can be obtained by a slightly longer cooking time. Vegetables should never be cooked for such a long time that they become mushy.

OTHER METHODS OF COOKING

Steaming
This method is successful with root vegetables and with marrows. It is a slow method of cooking. Vegetables tend to lose colour and there is a greater loss of Vitamin C than when vegetables are boiled.

Baking
Potatoes, onions and beetroots can be baked 'in their jackets' on a baking sheet or on an oven shelf. Vegetables cut into small pieces and wrapped into parcels with foil may be cooked in the oven. No water is needed, just put a knob of butter and salt and pepper in the parcel with the vegetables.

Roasting
Potatoes and vegetable marrow may be roasted in hot fat in a moderately hot oven. The dish may be covered but the vegetables will be crisper if left uncovered.

Cooking in fat
Vegetables may be cooked in just a little melted fat with no other liquid in a heavy saucepan with a tightly fitting lid, or in a sauté pan. Heat just a little fat, oil or butter, enough to cover the bottom of the pan. When it is just hot add the cut-up vegetables and seasoning. Put on the lid. Cook over gentle heat tossing the pan occasionally until the vegetables are tender. Aubergines, celery, carrots, parsnips, swedes, turnips and marrow are all suitable for this method.

Frying
Potatoes, sweet potatoes and plantains may be deep-fried. Potatoes, onions, tomatoes and mushrooms are among the vegetables suitable for shallow fat frying.

Pressure cooking
All vegetables may be cooked in a pressure cooker. This conserves more vitamins than any other method. Timing is important as if the cooking time is extended even briefly the vegetables will be overcooked. Check the manufacturer's advice for time of cooking each vegetable. Do not try to cook vegetables requiring different cooking times together.

COOKING PRESERVED VEGETABLES

Commercially frozen foods
These should be cooked according to the instructions on the packet. The same basic rules apply to frozen vegetables as to fresh. They should be put, preferably still frozen, into a pan containing a little boiling water. The pan should then be covered. Cooking time will be less than for fresh vegetables since in processing they will have been blanched or scalded before freezing. If you are already using the oven for other dishes the vegetables may be cooked there. This would save fuel. Put the vegetables on a piece of foil. Add a knob of butter and salt and pepper as necessary. Wrap up the vegetables into a parcel. Put on to a baking tin in the oven. A longer cooking time is needed than for boiling.

Canned vegetables
Canned vegetables are completely cooked in the canning process and only need reheating. Some of the soluble vitamins and minerals will have dissolved into the liquid in the can. The vegetables should be cooked in this liquid. If there is too much liquid it should be drained off the vegetables into a saucepan and boiled until some has evaporated. The vegetables may then be added and heated through. Drain the vegetables and save the surplus liquid.

Dried vegetables
Dried vegetables need a short or long period of soaking depending on the method of drying used. The vegetables should be cooked in the water in which they have been soaked.

TOOLS FOR VEGETABLE PREPARATION
There are dozens of tools and gadgets available which help to carry out, in varying degrees of efficiency, every process of vegetable preparation and cooking. Before buying any of these make sure you really need them. Many are expensive. Make sure that any of those you buy are easy to

use and to clean. The most labour-saving gadget is of no value if left unused in a drawer because it is too complicated to use or clean. Below are some of the basic tools you are most likely to need. You should have these before buying gadgets. Buy the best quality tools you can afford and look after them. Keep knives sharp. You are less likely to have an accident using a sharp knife than using one that is blunt.

Basic tools
Large, straightsided knife for chopping and
shredding cabbage
Medium-sized knife of the same shape for slicing
    carrots, mushrooms and tomatoes and for
    cutting up root vegetables
Small-sized knife for dicing and slicing vegetables
Potato peeler used also for peeling other vegetables
Chopping board of hardwood—wet vegetables
    will slip on very smooth surfaces like plastic
    laminate
Can opener
Colander
Vegetable rack
Vegetable brushes.

Gadgets
Here is a list of *gadgets* you may wish to purchase. Can you think of any others?
Onion holder
Mandolin
Ball maker
Chip potato cutter
Garlic press
Vegetable mill
Vegetable masher
Sieve
Salad basket
Tomato cutters and slicers
Spin-drier for lettuce
Bean slicer
Corn sticks
Automatic potato peeler
Juice separator
Asparagus pan
Chip pan and basket
Liquidizer.

Preservation

Since he first had a surplus to save, man has been concerned with the problem of preserving food in times of glut for use in times of shortage. Discoveries at prehistoric archaeological sites show that the earliest method of preservation was probably by drying and that cereals and pulses were the first foods treated in this way. Cereals and pulses will stay in good condition for years if kept dry and protected from insects and rodents.

The first really large-scale storage of food is probably that recorded in the Bible. Joseph, of the coat of many colours, organized the collection of surplus grain in the seven years of plentiful harvests to be used in the following seven years of famine. Over the centuries all the basic methods of preservation were discovered by trial and error.

The Ancient Egyptians found that fresh fruit rotted but would keep if dried in the sun. This method is still used. The Romans knew that ice would preserve food. Nero had food storage vaults in Rome kept cool by ice brought from the Alps. In the Middle Ages dried fruit, salted meat and fish, cured meats, vegetables and dried herbs were available. People built outside underground rooms which they filled with ice from rivers and lakes in the winter to help keep food fresh in spring and early summer. The Elizabethan era of exploration and long-distance voyagers brought new problems for the cook, who had to invent recipes for preserving all the food the sailors would need for the long weeks at sea, often in tropical regions.

About two hundred years ago inventors and scientists joined in efforts to make use of the accumulated knowledge and to undertake further research in order to revolutionize the basic methods. The French Government in 1795, concerned with the problems of feeding a vast army and navy, offered a prize of 12 000 francs for anyone who could invent a method of preserving food so that it remained wholesome for a long time. The prize was not claimed for fourteen years but in 1809 it was awarded to Nicolas Appert. He used wide-topped jars, heated them to drive off the air he thought caused deterioration and then put in a tightly fitting cork.

The following year an Englishman, Peter Durand, used as a container a metal canister based on the design of a tea canister, hence the term 'can'. These cans were expensive because they had to be hand made at the rate of about sixty a day; and because, like Appert, Durand did not know the scientific principles underlying canning, these cans frequently burst.

Various people tried to improve on this process but it was not until 1857 that Louis Pasteur discovered that it was not air but organisms called bacteria which caused the food to spoil.

Quick freezing is a discovery of this century. A young scientist, Clarence Birdseye, on a hunting trip in the Arctic, noticed that meat and fish frozen quickly in the keen arctic blizzards were tender and fresh when eaten months later. Food frozen slowly formed large ice crystals. These pierced the food cells so that when the food was later thawed the liquid nutrients leaked away leaving the food tough.

Each method of preservation used aimed to stop or slow down the natural processes of decay. Decay is caused by enzymes, yeasts, moulds and bacteria. These must be destroyed or rendered inactive.

Enzymes are chemical substances present in all living matter. In animals they bring about the processes of digestion. In plants they bring about the ripening of fruits. As soon as a plant is harvested enzymes encourage deterioration. They are highly sensitive to heat and destroyed by sterilization.

Yeasts are minute single-celled organisms which multiply by a process called budding. Yeast cells are always present in the air. They are susceptible to heat, being destroyed by exposure to a temperature of 75°C for a few minutes.

Moulds are common agents of spoilage in food. They are difficult to detect in the early stages of development. They start as fine thread-like forms called hypha. These multiply and interlace to form a mycelium which looks like cotton wool. Then vertical threads are produced and spores develop on the ends of these. The different colours of the spore—green, brown, black, etc.—give the different moulds their characteristic appearance. Enormous numbers of spores are produced. They are easily detached and carried away in the air. Each spore can produce a fresh growth of mould if it falls into a food which gives it suitable conditions for growth. Like yeasts, moulds are susceptible to heat, being easily destroyed by exposure to a temperature of 75°C for a few minutes.

Bacteria are the smallest and simplest forms of life. They are single-celled organisms which reproduce by dividing into two. Reproduction is very rapid. Under suitable conditions one cell develops into many millions of cells in a matter of hours. If conditions for the reproduction of normal vegetable cells are not suitable, certain types of bacteria can produce thick-walled cells called spores. The vegetative cells can be destroyed by heating for a short time at the temperature of boiling water, 100°C. The spores are more resistant to heat but they are susceptible to acids.

Different methods of preservation aim to destroy or inhibit the reproduction of these organisms.

1 *Chemical preservation*. Salt in large quantities makes conditions unsuitable for the growth of micro-organisms. Sugar in strong solutions of 40 to 50 per cent prevents the development of bacteria; certain yeasts and moulds are able to develop in even higher concentrations than this, hence the high proportion of sugar necessary for successful jam making. Vinegar can be used as a preservative because the active ingredient, acetic acid, prevents the development of micro-organisms.

2 *Drying*. This removes the moisture necessary for the growth of bacteria, yeasts and moulds.

3 *Bottling and canning* use heat treatment to destroy bacteria and enzymes.

4 *Freezing* prevents bacterial growth and slows down the action of enzymes.

DOMESTIC PRESERVATION OF VEGETABLES

Salting
French and runner beans are the only vegetables now thought suitable for salting and then only when there is a glut. The beans should be fresh and tender as salting tends to toughen them.

Basic method
1 Use large stoneware or glass containers.
2 Wash, dry and slice the beans in the usual way.
3 Put a thick layer of salt in the bottom of the container and then alternate layers of beans and salt.
4 Press each layer down well and finish with a salt layer.
5 Leave for a few days. The beans will shrink and liquid brine will form. The brine should not be removed.
6 Top up the jar with layers of beans and salt.
7 Cork or screw on lid. Make sure jar is air-tight.
8 Before beans are used they should be washed and soaked for two hours in warm water. Prolonged soaking causes toughness.

Pickling

This method is used to preserve onions, cauliflower, red cabbage, beetroot, gherkins, mushrooms and green tomatoes. The vegetables to be used should be in perfect condition. The best quality vinegar having a 5 per cent acetic acid content should be used. Wine vinegar gives a better appearance but malt vinegar a better taste. The vinegar is prepared by being cooked with mixed spices and sometimes sugar. It is used hot for vegetables you wish to soften and cold for those you wish to keep crisp.

Basic method

1 Vegetables are prepared by trimming and cutting into suitably sized pieces.
2 They are then covered in salt or soaked in brine for two or three days. This reduces the water content of the vegetables, toughens them and sometimes improves the colour. The salt is also a preservative.
3 The vegetables should be rinsed in cold water to remove all traces of salt.
4 Pack the vegetables loosely in jars to within 4 cm of the top.
5 Fill the jars with vinegar to 2 cm above the top of the vegetables.
6 Screw on the top of the jar.
7 The pickles should be stored for two to three months before use.

Bottling and Canning

Preserving vegetables by these methods is rather more difficult, and elaborate sterilizing equipment is necessary. It is not suitable for use in the average home. Anyone contemplating using this process should make a special study of the problems involved.

All vegetables may be heavily contaminated with soil organisms including the most heat-resistant form of bacteria. Unless these are killed by sterilization they may cause spoilage of the vegetables in the jar or can. These bacteria might cause more serious problems. Among the organisms may be one called *Bacillus botulinus*. The spores of this, if not destroyed, can develop and form a toxin which can cause serious and often rapidly fatal food-poisoning. There might be no discolouration or bad smell to warn you of the danger in eating the vegetables.

Fruits and tomatoes can safely be bottled and canned at home because they are acid. This acidity inhibits the growth of the organisms and prevents the formation of its toxin.

Non-acid foods must be processed by being packed into sealed containers and heated at 122°C for 30 to 40 minutes.

Freezing

Food must be frozen at a temperature below −21°C. At this temperature enzyme action is slowed down so that the food stays in good condition for a long period. Home freezing cannot be done in the ice-box of a refrigerator or in a conservator. Only a deep-freeze cabinet can provide sufficiently low temperature. Most vegetables can be frozen successfully, the exception being those which have a high water content and are usually eaten new and crisp. These include salad greens, radishes, cucumbers and tomatoes. Cabbage can be frozen if it is to be served cooked.

Basic method

1 Absolute cleanliness is essential. Freezing does not kill all micro-organisms. Some are only prevented from growth while they are in the freezer.
2 Choose vegetables in perfect condition. Freezing cannot improve poor food.
3 Thoroughly wash the vegetables. Trim off bruised and wilted parts.
4 Sort them as to size because larger pieces need longer blanching than small pieces.
5 If any vegetable is normally sliced or cut before cooking it is usual to do this before freezing.
6 Vegetables should be blanched by being submerged for several minutes in water kept at boiling point. The time varies according to the vegetable. Blanching prevents off-flavours developing, preserves the texture and prevents the quick loss of ascorbic acid during storage. These changes are caused by enzymes. These enzymes must be destroyed before freezing and the short blanching or scalding does this. Timing of blanching should be accurate. Under-blanching will not destroy the enzymes while over-blanching will cook the vegetables so that when served they will look like leftovers of a poor colour and texture and be low in vitamin content.
7 The moment blanching is complete the vegetables should be chilled rapidly, preferably

by being put into a wire basket and plunged into a large pan of chilled water. This process quickly stops the vegetables cooking and should continue for at least as long as the blanching time, often longer. Test a few pieces to make sure that they are cool in the centre.

8 Drain and pack the vegetables immediately.
9 To make a solid pack merely put the vegetables in a container leaving head space.
10 Seal and freeze.
11 If you are likely to need only a portion of each package at a time it is easier to be able to 'pour' out some of the vegetables. After draining the vegetables spread them out in a single layer on trays and put them in the freezer. When they are frozen hard, pack the loose vegetables in containers leaving no head space. Seal and freeze.

COMMERCIAL PRESERVATION OF VEGETABLES

Commercial preservation is based on the traditional domestic methods differing basically only in the quantity processed. The whole process is streamlined and automation used whenever possible.

Food preservation on a commercial scale is one of the newest, fastest growing industries. In many areas of the country farmers are under direct contract to the food industry. Standardization is essential to the food industry at every stage. Farmers are told what varieties to grow, when seeding must take place and what fertilizers to use. Experts measure the heat of the soil to decide the best time for sowing seed. This is staggered so that there is a continuous flow of vegetables to the factory. This flow is at the rate at which the factory can process the food, without it being delayed even for hours. Some foods are completely processed within an hour of being picked. At harvest time the crops are checked for readiness by food technologists. No crops are gathered until they are perfect for processing. To make sure that there is no delay between cropping and processing, operatives on the farm may be in radio contact with the factory. Crops are harvested only when the factory is ready to deal with them. Sometimes even the harvesting machinery is owned by the factory and the operator employed by them on contract.

Canning
In the canning factory the following processes are carried out, most of them mechanically.
1 The vegetables are cleaned and prepared.
2 They are blanched by being passed through boiling water or through a tunnel into which steam is injected. They travel at the precise speed which ensures that they are blanched for exactly the right length of time.
3 They are passed on a conveyor belt to the automatic weighing machines. Another conveyor belt brings the washed, open cans ready to be filled.
4 The correct quantity of food is weighed and put into each can.
5 The appropriate quantity of liquid is poured into each can.
6 Lids are fitted to the can. All the air is drawn out of the can and it is sealed.
7 The cans are then passed into a sterilizing machine. Sterilization under pressure destroys the most heat-resistant bacteria. The time taken depends on the size of the can and the acidity of the contents.
8 Cans are cooled by gradually reducing the pressure and then allowing the temperature to fall slowly.
9 Cans are labelled automatically and are then conveyed to the packing section where they are boxed ready for storage and distribution.

Freezing
In the frozen-food factory food is processed in the same way as for domestic freezing but this is carried out automatically. The food is frozen by three methods.
1 *Immersion freezing.* Food is plunged into a very cold solution. For vegetables this may be an invert sugar solution.
2 *Convection freezing.* A blast of cold air is directed into the food, quickly freezing it.
3 *Multiplate freezer.* This is a cabinet with a number of hollow shelves which form the freezing surfaces. The food is placed between the shelves and the shelves pressed together on to the food.

Food is frozen at a lower temperature than in a domestic freezer; usually at $-25°C$ to $-35°C$. Once the food is frozen this low temperature is not necessary. Storage rooms are maintained at $-20°C$. Workers in storage rooms must wear special protective clothing and only work in the rooms for short periods at a time.

Dehydration

Dehydration is basically the same as the first method of food preservation carried out by man. The Second World War started the technological advances which have led to the popularity of this method. It is an important means of preservation because it produces foods which are light, easily transported and, if correctly packaged, need no special storage conditions. The most usual system of drying is by hot air. The particles of food are kept in motion to speed up the process and prevent the small pieces sticking together.

Other driers include the drum driers in which food is spread over heated rollers (used for potato flakes) and spray driers in which the food is dispersed as droplets into the drying air (tomatoes).

In accelerated freeze-drying the foodstuff is first frozen so that the natural moisture in it is turned into ice. It is then placed in a chamber under high vacuum and heated. The ice evaporates directly without turning back into moisture. By AFD the texture and quality of the food is maintained so that when the food is unpacked and moisture added the food has a good flavour and quality.

Whichever method of drying is used the food must still be washed, trimmed, blanched and chilled before processing. Packing is very important. Moisture must be kept out of the packs so complete sealing is essential.

The food industry

Since the start of the Industrial Revolution and the population shift from country to town, the problems of the growing and distribution of food have increased. At first it was a matter of too little manpower to farm the land efficiently, and of the distances produce had to be carried to reach the consumer. By the time fruit and vegetables reached the towns they were often stale and expensive. You could only purchase vegetables which had been grown a comparatively short distance from your home. Most town dwellers had nowhere to grow the vegetables and herbs produced in most cottage gardens.

The wealthy might have spent their time consuming huge meals but for the majority just getting enough to survive was a problem. Malnutrition was widespread. The standard of hygiene was low. The problem of food wastage is too high even today. In the past, with the difficulties of rodent and insect control, and lack of suitable transport and storage facilities, a very much larger quantity of food was wasted or was a potential source of food poisoning.

As industrialization increased so did mechanization. The railways carried goods and produce as well as passengers. Machinery was designed and made to ease the labour problems on the land. Refrigerated ships and railway wagons could take

food long distances in good condition. New branches of technology and food science developed and industries grew to support and integrate the new innovations and inventions.

Food production increased as the land available for agriculture lessened. The very roads and railways which took produce from the farms to the consumer were using up vast areas of land. These inroads continue to the present day but at least people are now aware of the danger.

People are not satisfied with a meagre diet or with a lack of variety in food. Home-grown crops are supplemented by food purchased from overseas. This uses up a good deal of the national income. The developing countries are beginning to use increasing quantities of their own food for their own people.

Modern methods of food preservation form an important part of the pattern. Mass preservation saves wastage. Perishable foods are processed at their prime and can be kept in store until needed. It is now possible to eat spring and summer crops all the year round. If there is a glut of food it can be saved for a time of shortage instead of being ploughed back into the ground.

If food is to be processed in large economical quantities there must be a large-scale production of food. Farmers with small farms cannot always compete. Very expensive machinery is needed. To use this machinery efficiently fields must be large, and hedges which may be centuries old have to be removed. This destroys the habitat of much wild life. Birds which live on insects no longer have nesting places so insecticides have to be used. Lack of hedging can lead to 'dust bowl' conditions. In East Anglia farmers are finding that high winds unchecked by hedges and other windbreaks are drying out the soil too quickly. The fine top soil is blown away together with the seeds and fertilizer, often clogging up irrigation ditches. This means that second seeding and more fertilizer may be needed. The balance and texture of the soil is upset and it is likely to be years before it rights itself. Farmers are now reluctant to remove windbreaks and are indeed replanting hedges to replace those scrapped a few years ago.

On the credit side there is the advantage of regular supplies of food in excellent condition and at reasonable prices. In addition the food industry finances a range of research projects on efficient farming, plant genetics, and new means of preserving and storing food. Plant wastage is kept to a minimum in food factories. It is recycled into human and animal foods, made into fertilizers, used as a source of a variety of drugs for the food industry, medicinal drugs and for dyes, building materials and paint, among numerous other uses. Plants contain protein. This can be extracted from plant waste as well as from specially grown crops. This leaf protein is very important to a protein hungry world.

Many ancillary industries and professions have developed to cope with the needs of the food industry. Millions of people work here and overseas to try to satisfy the appetite of the wealthier nations and to improve the lot of those in underdeveloped areas. Farming is no longer a matter of a farmer with a horse-drawn plough selling his products directly to the consumer. It is a world-wide highly organized industry. Here are just a few aspects (remember that each involves other industries, crafts, trades and professions all interdependent):

Research and teaching at research stations, universities, polytechnics, agricultural and horticultural colleges

Research on soil, insects, plants, plant diseases, irrigation, nutrition and dietetics

Design and production of agricultural equipment and machinery

Seed and plant production

Research on and production of fertilizers, insecticides and herbicides

Builders of glasshouses, factories, food stores

Heating engineers

The growers—farmers and horticulturists

Meteorologists who give farmers advance notice of weather conditions

The frozen, canned and dried-food industries

Packaging—metal, plastics, paper, cartons, tins, bags and sacks

Publishers and printers—instruction books, trade magazines, recipe development

Publicity in television, radio, magazines and newspapers

Brokers and buyers, world-wide, wholesale and retail

Sales and distribution from seeds, books and equipment to the final product

Transport workers on ships, railways and lorries

Workers in the retail trade selling the produce to the consumer.

Vegetables A to Z

ARTICHOKE, GLOBE

The globe artichoke is the edible green flower bud of a plant of the thistle family. Regarded as a luxury plant, it is very easily grown in this country, and attractive enough to plant in a flower bed. The plant has dusty, silvery green foliage. There are purple and green varieties, the former having sharper spikes.

A popular plant for cooks in this country a century ago, it went out of favour in the kitchen and kitchen garden, but has recently reappeared on the market as an exotic import. Most artichokes sold by greengrocers are imported from Brittany but the plant originated in the Middle East. The edible part of the plant is the bud made up of green overlapping fleshy leaves. These cover a tough hairy choke. Below the choke is the 'fond' or tender heart.

Available: home produced—June to August; foreign—March to November (imported from France, Israel, Italy, Spain).

Shopping. A good artichoke should be heavy for its size. The leaves should be in good condition without spots or streaks. They should be tight and compact. If the leaves are spreading apart the artichoke is old. There should be about 15 cm of stem left attached to the bud. This is important as the stem holds water which helps to keep the bud in good condition during transportation,

marketing and storage. Use as soon as possible after harvesting. A really fresh bud will keep for up to a week if left unwashed, wrapped in plastic film in a really cool larder or refrigerator.

To eat. Many people refuse artichokes because they do not know how to eat them. There is really nothing complicated to learn.
1 Pull leaves off one at a time by hand.
2 Dip the fleshy base of the leaf into the sauce or dressing.
3 Suck or scrape the pulp of the edible base of the leaf between the teeth. The upper part of the leaf is inedible. Leave the stripped leaf on the side of the plate.
4 When all the leaves have been removed the hairy choke can be seen easily. This is inedible. Scoop it out with a teaspoon and put this with the stripped leaves on the side of the plate.
5 The heart which is left is the most nourishing and most highly flavoured part of the bud. This should be eaten, using a knife and fork.

Cultivation. Sow seed in March or April. Set out the plants in June. Allow them plenty of space as they will grow to a metre across. Roots can be purchased for April planting. They need rich soil and a sunny well-drained place. Do not expect a crop in the first year. If they do produce buds the first year clip off the buds when small leaving only one or two. You will eventually have dozens of heads. Divide the roots every year.

ARTICHOKE, JERUSALEM

The Jerusalem artichoke is a tuber which looks rather like a new potato covered with warty 'knobs'. Indigenous to North America where it grows wild, it was cultivated by very early North American Indians. It first reached Europe at the start of the seventeenth century as an exotic luxury.

There are several versions of how it got its name. The artichoke part came about because its flavour resembles that of the globe artichoke. Jerusalem is said to be the corruption of the Italian word for sunflower, 'girasole', which the plant and its flower resembles. A more likely explanation is that it derives from the English street hawkers' cry of the name of the place in Holland where the plants were first grown, Ter Neasan.

It was popular in the seventeenth and eighteenth centuries. It probably fell out of favour because most of the recipes ensured that prolonged cooking spoiled the texture, and sauces masked the delicate flavour. In the Eastern Mediterranean the Jerusalem artichoke is treated like a potato and eaten with everything, even as a sweet course. There are several varieties, some having red or purple tinted tubers but the most popular are those with pale cream skin ringed with pink. They are easily grown in this country.

Available: home produced and foreign—September and May (imported from France and Holland).

Shopping and storage. Avoid misshapen or small tubers and any that are extra dirty or bruised. They should be firm, not flabby or wrinkled. Store in a vegetable rack in a cool place.

Cultivation. Plant the tubers in February and March 10 cm deep, 30 cm apart. Harvest them from the start of October right through the winter, leaving the tubers in the ground until they are needed. They will not be harmed by frost which actually improves the flavour.

ASPARAGUS

The name is of Greek origin, and the vegetable was familiar to both ancient Greeks and Romans, though there appears to have been frequent confusion between asparagus and broccoli. The plant grows wild where the soil and air is impregnated with salt, in Europe, Asia Minor and the Mediterranean area. It can grow up to three metres high but it is for the young spears or shoots that the plant is cultivated in warm and temperate regions of Europe and America.

Available: home produced—May to July; foreign—January to May (imported from Belgium, Cyprus, France, Israel and USA).

Shopping and storage. Care should be taken when choosing asparagus. Home produced plants have a short season and the asparagus is expensive. Imported bunches are available for a longer season. However, because of the time taken in transit they are not always of such good quality as locally grown varieties. The spears are sold by weight or in bundles. The heads should be close and compact on fairly thick stalks 20 to 25 cm high. Do not purchase bent, split or dried out shoots. Very thin stalks known as sprue appear at the end of the season. These are less expensive but may be coarse and of less delicate flavour than the main crop. Asparagus wilts quickly, and should be used on the day of purchase. It can be revived to a certain extent by standing up to the neck in cold water for a short time.

To eat asparagus. If served alone with melted butter, asparagus should be picked up with the fingers. Pick up each stick by the stalk end. The tips and tender part of the stem is eaten. The coarse lower stems should be returned unobtrusively to the side of the plate. If asparagus is served as a vegetable with meat or other food it can be taken with a knife and fork.

Cultivation. Asparagus plants are not difficult to grow but you will not be able to harvest a crop until the plant is at least three years old. The ground needs careful preparation. Deep digging and plentiful manuring are essential. Asparagus likes light, well drained, alkaline soil. Purchase one-year-old crowns as these are easiest to establish and give long-term dividends. Plant the crowns in rows one metre apart with 30 to 40 cm between plants.

AUBERGINE (egg plant)

The aubergine is of the same botanical family as the potato and the tomato. It originated in India and soon became an important vegetable in Middle-Eastern cookery. There are many different varieties. They may be elongated, pear-shaped or round, and vary in colouring from pale greyish violet to deepest purple. The deep purple/black fruit, about 20 cm long is the most popular in this country.

Available: foreign—January to November (imported from the Canary Islands, France, Israel, Italy and Kenya).

Shopping and storage. The fruit (botanically a berry) should be glossy, plump and firm. Soft, shrunken fruits have started to decay. For stuffing, choose the long pear-shaped variety. The round type are easier to dice. A really fresh aubergine should store for up to a week in a refrigerator before deterioration starts.

Cultivation. They can be grown in this country in a warm greenhouse or conservatory or even on a window sill. Grow them as you would tomatoes. Sow seeds singly in 6 cm pots at a temperature of 18°C (65°F). When the plant has a second pair of leaves it should be transferred to a 15 cm pot. Keep the plants well watered and give them an occasional spray of water on top especially when in flower as this 'sets' the fruit.

AVOCADO PEAR (Known also as alligator pear, custard apple, butter pear or midshipman's marrow)

This is a staple food in many Latin-American countries. It is known as a pear because of its shape. It is a very recent import into this country—in 1960 the first avocados were imported from Israel. Now they are obtained fairly easily during the season. There are four main varieties:
Ettinger—bright green with shiny smooth skins
Fuerte—bright green with slightly rough skins
Hass—rough purplish brown skins
Nabal—large and round with slightly rough green skins
The golden yellow flesh has a nutty flavour and a creamy smooth consistency.

Available: foreign—September to May (imported from Israel, South Africa, USA).

Shopping and storage. You can only judge an avocado by the feel. Cradle it gently in the palm of your hand. If it is ready to eat it will yield to gentle pressure. Be careful when buying avocado pears. The fruit is shipped in an under-ripe condition and it is often difficult to purchase a perfectly ripe avocado pear. Buy unripe pears several days before you intend to use them. They will then stay in good condition in a refrigerator for a week or, if they are already ripe, for three or four days. If you wish to hasten the ripening wrap them individually in newspaper and put them in a plastic bag or box. They will ripen in a day or two in a warm room.

Cultivation. You are unlikely to be able to grow your own pears as the plant bears fruit only in a hot climate but you can grow an attractive indoor foliage plant. Nick the base of the stone in the form of a cross. Stick toothpicks into the stone around the middle and suspend it in a glass with its base in water. Put the glass in a moderately warm place. Rooting can take several months so do not forget to keep the water topped up. When the roots show, plant the stone in a flower pot of sandy loam. Keep the soil moist but well-drained.

BEANS

There are thousands of varieties of beans developed from the few original kinds known to have been cultivated over 10 000 years ago. Every civilization has had its own special bean. Europe's bean, the broad bean, has the longest known history. It was first cultivated around the Caspian Sea. The ancient Greeks had a God of Beans and held Bean Feasts in honour of Apollo. Findings in the Iron Age 'lake dwellings' at Glastonbury show that they were cultivated and eaten in considerable quantities. The French bean originally came from South America and about a thousand dwarf and climbing varieties have been developed. Two varieties of runner bean, white and scarlet, are grown in Britain. They are related to the French bean and also originated in South America.

Throughout the centuries the bean has been valued as a food which could not only be eaten fresh but also dried and stored for use during winter, famine and a time of crop failure. It is a useful source of vegetable protein and particularly useful in the diet of people who do not eat animal proteins. French and runner beans freeze well. Broad, French and runner beans are those most often used in Britain. Not all beans are green podded. There are violet-mottled French beans, beans with purple stems and foliage but blue pods, and yellow podded beans. These and other novelties are as easily grown as the usual varieties. Details of them are found in many seedsmen's catalogues.

Broad Beans
Available: home produced—June to September; foreign—April to June (imported from France, Canary Islands, Italy, Spain).

Shopping and storage. At the beginning of the season the very young beans are so tender that they can be eaten whole. Later the shell coarsens and only the beans inside can be used so a larger quantity must be purchased. Avoid beans where the stem and pod have darkened to dark brown or black as this is a sign of age. Pods should not be flabby but well filled yet not tight and hard. The age of the bean is important as it determines the way it is to be cooked and served.

Cultivation. Broad beans are more hardy than any other bean. The seed can even be sown in the autumn in mild areas where the plants will live through the winter without protection. Otherwise sow as early as February or early March. Sow in a sunny position. Beans do well in heavy clay soil. Sow beans 8 cm deep in carefully prepared soil of fine tilth in drills 50 cm apart at intervals of 25 cm, or in staggered rows 25 cm apart. Taller varieties need the support of stakes, or of strings or nets fixed to strong supports. Water plentifully. Feed occasionally. Pinch out growing tips when the flowers have set. Pick beans frequently to encourage further production.

French Beans
Available: home produced—June to September; foreign—April to June (imported from France, Canary Islands, Italy, Spain).

Shopping and storage. Modern varieties are almost stringless but it is sensible to avoid coarse looking specimens. They should be crisp, straight and flat, not showing the beans inside. They do not keep well but will remain crisp overnight if wrapped in a damp cloth.

Cultivation: French beans are vulnerable to frost so should not be planted too early in the year. Wait until all danger of night frost is over or arrange for frost protection at night. Sow in early May and make successional sowing every two weeks until late June. Choose a sunny location. Soil should be well prepared. Sow in rows 50 cm apart, 5 cm deep and the seeds 12 to 15 cm apart. Thin young plants to 20 to 25 cm apart. The dwarf varieties do not need staking. Harvest when beans are young and tender before the seeds are ripe and the pods coarsen.

Runner Beans
Available: home produced—June to September;

foreign—April to June (imported from France, Canary Islands, Italy, Spain).

Shopping and storage. If possible grow beans in the garden as they very quickly dry off after picking. Runner beans tend to be stringy. Fresh beans should be crisp and snap easily. Do not purchase beans when the shape of the seed shows through the pod. Cook as soon as possible after picking without storing. If necessary, a short soak in cold water will restore some crispness. Runner beans can be purchased frozen or easily frozen at home.

Cultivation. These are the hungriest of all the beans so the soil should be well prepared by double digging and by working plenty of well rotted manure or garden compost into the bottom spit. Sow seed from May to late June in drills 5 cm deep with 15 to 30 cm between the plants. The seeds can be sown in a circle around long poles arranged wigwam fashion and tied securely together at the top. Pinch off the growing tip of the plant when it reaches the top of the support. Harvest frequently. This is a high yielding crop.

BEAN SPROUTS (mung and soya beans)
These are being used increasingly in Britain, as people become interested in Chinese food, as well as by the people from the East who live in this country. Bean sprouts are usually grown from mung or soya beans.

Available: home produced—throughout the year.

Shopping and storage. Bean sprouts are usually sold fresh in shops which specialize in selling Chinese foodstuffs. They can be purchased in tins but are very easy to grow at home. If you purchase fresh sprouts and do not wish to use them immediately, put them into a container with a tightly fitting lid and store them in a refrigerator for up to four days.

Cultivation. Soak the beans for about six hours before 'sowing'. Put the soaked beans on to a piece of damp flannel or pad of moist tissues on a dish. Keep the dish in a completely dark place where the temperature stays at a steady 13°C. Water daily. Harvest your crop 72 to 90 hours later when the vitamin, mineral salt and enzyme content is highest. By then the roots are 5 cm long and two pointed leaves are emerging.

BEETROOT

Probably first cultivated in the Mediterranean region, the beetroot grows wild from there to as far as Persia and the Caspian Sea. It was well known at least two thousand years ago but then only the leaves were used as food, the roots being employed medicinally. They have never had the popularity they deserve in Britain. In Poland, Russia and other Eastern European countries they are an important ingredient of many dishes, especially of borsch, a beetroot soup. In the USA they are served both hot and cold and as a salad ingredient. Apart from the the familiar dark red beetroots there are white and gold varieties and both round and long shapes.

Available: home produced—all the year round starting about June; foreign (imported from Scandinavia, Poland, Denmark and Holland).

Shopping and storage. Beetroots may be purchased raw or ready cooked. Early beetroots are sold in small bunches of small roots. As they get larger they are sold loose. Avoid large roots as they are likely to be coarse and fibrous. They will store well in a cool place for a week to ten days but once cooked should be used within a day or two. When handling beetroot wear rubber or plastic gloves or your hands will be stained pink for days.

Cultivation. Beetroots are easily grown and if successive sowings are made at monthly intervals from April onwards you can harvest small roots throughout the summer. July sowing will provide roots for autumn and winter. Sow in drills 20 mm deep, 40 cm apart in clusters of two or three seeds 15 to 25 cm apart. Later thin seedlings leaving one in each position. Water well. Start lifting roots in July taking care not to damage them. They can be stored in sand for winter use or can be frozen.

BROCCOLI

Broccoli is a member of the cabbage family and is closely related to the cauliflower and similar to it in appearance. However, instead of producing one head it has a number of long thin stems each with a small curd or underdeveloped floret head surrounded by green elongated leaves.

Available: sprouting broccoli (white and purple)—February to April; calabrese (green Italian)—July until the autumn frosts.

Shopping and storage. Choose fresh young shoots with firm stems which snap easily. Use as soon as possible after purchase or picking. Italian calabrese, the green sprouting broccoli, is ideal for freezing.

Cultivation. See under *Cabbage.*

BRUSSELS SPROUTS

The Brussels sprout is a comparatively new species of cabbage, developed only 500 years ago. It was introduced to this country from Brussels in the nineteenth century.

Available: home produced—August to March.

Shopping and storage: Fresh sprouts will be tight and dark green in colour though occasional red ones may be found. Small or medium-sized sprouts are more likely to be free from internal blemish than the large ones. Small tight samples are more expensive than the looser ones but there is no waste to them. When the weather is warm in late summer and early autumn the first crops of sprouts may be loose leaved. Sprouts are now the most popular of frozen vegetables sold in even larger quantities than the pea.

Cultivation. Sow thinly in drills 2 cm deep and 25 cm apart in March. In April and May plant out the seedlings a metre apart. (Fill gaps with lettuce or early cabbage plants.) Water well and feed occasionally. Large plants may need staking. Gather sprouts from the bottom of the stems first. Leave the tops until all the sprouts have been picked, usually in February, when they will make a useful green vegetable.

CABBAGE

There are numerous branches of the cabbage family including cauliflowers, Brussels sprouts, kale and broccoli. They all originate from the two well-known types, both green, one with smooth leaves and the other with curly leaves. From these many hybrid varieties have been developed.

The cabbage is a native of Western Asia and Europe. It has been cultivated for its leaves throughout Europe since the earliest times. Important work in developing improved strains has been carried out in England since the sixteenth century.

Available: home produced and foreign—throughout the year (imported from France and Holland).

69

Shopping. Different types are available at different overlapping periods of the year. They are seldom named in the shops so you need to be aware of the appearance and main seasons of each type.

Spring cabbage
(available from November to April)
This is a misleading name as spring cabbage is available during the winter when it is sold under the name of spring greens before the hearts have developed. Hearted cabbages, which are generally available in spring, are conical or pointed towards the centre. Spring cabbage should be a deep green colour and look crisp. It is tender, succulent and well flavoured. If used fresh every bit can be eaten so there is no wastage.

Summer and autumn cabbages
(available from June to October)
Choose firm solid heads with clean undamaged outer leaves. They are less liable to damage than spring greens.

Savoy (available from August to early spring)
The dark green, round, hard heads have crinkled or blistered looking outer leaves. They are big, an average savoy weighs from 1.5 to 2 kg, though they would be smaller than this early in the season. They are very hardy and can stand severe frosts. They are sometimes sold with layers of ice between the leaves and should then be slowly defrosted in cold water.

White cabbage
(available from October to February)
A round, solid cabbage which is pale green, almost white in colour. It can be cooked but is better finely shredded and eaten raw mixed with other salad vegetables or tossed in salad dressing.

Red cabbage (available from autumn to spring)
This differs from green cabbage only in colour. The dark purple-red, smooth leaves turn a dramatic crimson when cooked with something acid such as lemon juice or vinegar, otherwise the colour is lost and it turns grey. Choose compact heads, not too large as the leaves are usually densely packed. Do not buy heads with damaged spots or split stems. As well as being cooked, cabbage can be served raw in salads and as a pickle. It is widely used in Germany and other central European countries and is gaining favour, especially for pickling, in this country.

Winter cabbage
(available from Christmas to March)
The drumhead varieties, in season throughout the year though expensive in the spring, are the most favoured winter cabbages. They are smooth, round and compact and should have no yellowish tinge. Avoid those where a thick stalk penetrates far up into the head as you would be paying for stalk, not cabbage.

Shopping and storage. Spring greens are sold by weight. Heads are sold individually but priced by weight. Make sure the cabbage is fresh. If you cook it properly as soon as possible or, better still, eat it raw, it is an excellent source of Vitamin C. If offered half a large cabbage, you should refuse it as there will be considerable loss of Vitamin C from the cut surfaces. Look for firm heads and healthy looking leaves. The cabbage should smell sweet, be sound and look good enough to eat raw. Avoid those which have had their outer leaves removed. They might have been taken off because they were stale and withered. The stalk should be fresh and moist not dry and cracked. Cabbage should be eaten as soon as possible after harvesting to gain the maximum amount of Vitamin C. Avoid storage but if necessary do so for the shortest possible time. Cabbage must be kept cool, away from light and wrapped to prevent loss of moisture. A plastic bag or box in a refrigerator is best for this but if you do not have a refrigerator, wrap the cabbage in a clean cloth and put it in a tin or saucepan with a tight lid in a cool place. Before storing remove damaged leaves and trim a little off the end of the stalk. Do not over-trim the stalk as this contains moisture which helps to keep the vegetable fresh.

Cultivation. Sow autumn and winter cabbage outdoors from March to May and plant out from May to June. Sow spring cabbage outdoors from mid-June to mid-August, planting out in September and October. Space out the seedlings 45 cm apart in rows 60 cm apart.

CAPSICUM, see PEPPERS

CARROTS
The carrot, a member of the parsley family, probably originated in Afghanistan in prehistoric times. It has been cultivated in the Mediterranean area since several centuries BC but it was probably grown as a herb for its scented foliage rather than for the root. It was introduced to this country by

immigrants from Holland in the time of Elizabeth I. There are red, white and purple varieties but we usually eat the bright orange type. Apart from its medicinal use it can be dried and ground for use as a coffee substitute, eaten raw or cooked, used in soups, salads, cakes and jam. It has become a basic vegetable for cooks throughout Europe and America.

Available: home produced—throughout the year; foreign—January to July (imported from Canada, Cyprus, Holland, Israel, Italy, USA).

Shopping and storage. Avoid very large carrots as they are likely to have a lot of useless core. Split or broken carrots will deteriorate quickly. Carrots should be well shaped, smooth skinned and of a good bright colour. A good quality carrot should snap cleanly in the fingers. The best carrots are about as thick as a man's thumb with no green in the crown. Young carrots are sold in bunches and main crop, with foliage trimmed, are sold loose. Buy little and often. Main crops can be stored for a week or so if kept in a well ventilated part of a cool, dry cupboard. If they are to be stored in a refrigerator the green tops should be removed and the roots put into a plastic bag or into the vegetable section. Unwashed carrots store better than washed ones and only those in tip top condition should be kept. For home freezing use young carrots.

Cultivation. A sunny position is best for early crops. Sow at intervals from April to mid-July in 1 cm deep drills 30 cm apart. Thin out seedlings to 10 to 20 cm apart. Pull from June onwards. If you delay thinning until the young carrots are just large enough to be eaten you will get the most out of your sowing.

CAULIFLOWER

The cauliflower is a variety of cabbage cultivated for its under-developed flower, not for its leaves. It is believed to have originated in Cyprus, to have been introduced to Italy in the sixteenth century and to have reached Britain as late as the early nineteenth century. Centuries of cultivation have resulted in many varieties being available throughout the year, apart from temporary shortages during spells of bad weather.

Available: home produced—throughout the year; foreign—January to March, June, November to December.

Shopping and storage. Cauliflower is most plentiful and least expensive between June and October. Winter cauliflower, which used to be known as winter broccoli, tends to have leaves folded over the curd to protect it from the cold. Summer varieties are more open. Choose heads with a thick white curd and crisp green leaves. Yellowish curds, caused by too much sun, rain or frost, are less attractive in appearance. The flavour is not affected by the discolouration and the heads are often sold off cheaply so these could be a worth-while purchase. Avoid loose-spreading curds and those with brown marks. Never buy any with yellowed leaves as this is a sign of deterioration. Use the cauliflower as soon as possible after purchase or cutting. Leave the coarse leaf stalks on the head during storage. Cut a thin slice off the butt end but avoid overtrimming because the butt contains moisture which helps keep the head fresh longer. If you have a very large cauliflower and need only a part of it cut off the leaf stalks as necessary and break off the flowerets from the head. Leave the butt on any used part to be stored.

Cultivation. Early crops should be sown under glass in a temperature of 13°C in February and, after hardening, planted out 60 cm apart. The main summer crops can be sown directly outside in a seed bed 1 cm deep in April and May, and the early spring crops in August. The young plants should be transplanted to 60 cm apart.

CELERIAC

Celeriac is a member of the celery family. Originally a Mediterranean plant, it gradually spread over Europe. It was introduced into Britain in the eighteenth century. It is very popular in France and Germany but not given the importance it deserves in this country.

Unlike celery which is grown for its stems, celeriac is a swollen root stem sometimes called turnip-rooted. It looks rather like a battered coconut with the hairs removed and has a brown skin with an uneven surface. It has the flavour of celery and can be used for many recipes usually made with celery. The white flesh is of a more solid texture and will keep in store for much longer than celery.

Available: home produced—October to April.

Shopping and storage. See that the roots are firm and heavy for their size. Avoid rotting or damaged samples. If the root is too large for one meal, you can use part and save the rest for next day. The flesh discolours when exposed to air so cover the part you intend to save immediately you cut the root. Celeriac can be stored in a cool dry place for use throughout the winter.

Cultivation. Celeriac is easier to grow than celery. Sow the seed in February and March in boxes or under glass at a temperature of 13°C. Prick out when large enough to handle. Plant out at intervals of 30 cm in rich soil.

CELERY
A native of Europe, it probably originated in the Mediterranean area. The plant, a weed common to Europe, started its cultivated career as a medicinal herb and was still used as such in the sixteenth century. During the seventeenth century it was improved by Italian gardeners to resemble the vegetable we eat today. There are now two main kinds, the ordinary main crop which must be blanched during growth and a self-blanching variety.

Available: home produced—August to February; foreign—January to July (imported from the Canary Islands, Holland, Israel, USA).

Shopping and storage. Available generally in white and green forms. Much celery is now sold pre-washed and pre-packed. Pre-washed celery often has soil left clinging to it. Washed celery goes limp more quickly than celery left unwashed. Celery sold with all the tops removed may be stale since one of the signs of this is the yellowing and wilting of the leaves. Celery is sold by the head and will vary in size and price. Very small heads may be all leaves and no heart. Avoid those with leaves split or swollen at the base as this might be the work of burrowing insects. Before storing, remove discoloured leaves and stalks and brush off loose soil.

Cultivation. Celery seeds germinate very slowly so it is best to grow young plants under glass in a temperature of 13°C. Prick out when large enough to handle. Plant out self-blanching varieties 30 cm apart in rich soil. Main-crop plants should be planted in rich soil in a trench 30 cm wide and 50 cm deep. When the plants are 30 cm high they should be gradually earthed up each week leaving only the top tufts of leaves exposed.

CELTUCE
An unusual combination of celery and lettuce.

Although belonging to the lettuce family the leaves of celtuce have four times the Vitamin C content of lettuce. A very useful plant with lettuce-like leaves and a heart or stems like celery. Both can be eaten raw or cooked.

Available: home produced—August to February.

Shopping and storage. Not often seen for sale in a greengrocer's shop. Avoid heads with limp leaves and stems, or stems with brown discolouration. Use as soon as possible, especially the leaves. If you have to store celtuce do so in a cool vegetable rack or a refrigerator. Remove discoloured leaves and damaged stalks.

Cultivation. A very easy vegetable to grow. Sow thinly from late April onward in rows 10 mm deep with 30 cm between the rows. Later thin plants out to 25 cm apart.

CHARD
Also known as leaf chard, leaf beet, Swiss chard, seakale beet, silver beet. These names are given to a variety of beetroots cultivated for the chards or midribs rather than the roots. The plant has long fleshy stalks each topped with a spinach like leaf. The leaves may be treated like spinach; the stalks tied in bundles and cooked like asparagus or seakale.

Available: home produced—November to May.

CHICORY
Chicory is often confused with endive although they are quite different in appearance. What we call chicory is in France and the USA called endive. In Belgium it is called chicory in the market but endive when cooked. Chicory is the more versatile of the two vegetables. It can be eaten raw or cooked in many ways. It grows wild in many places in Europe, Russia, Kashmir and the Punjab. It is a tall slender plant with blue flowers attractive enough to cultivate in the flower garden for decorative purposes. The plant is used as the bitter component of many continental coffees. In much of Europe roots of the Witloof variety are used as a vegetable. The cultivation of the plant we know today did not start until about 1845 when market gardeners near Brussels first began to blanch it like celery. Belgium is still the largest producer in Europe.

Available: home grown—September to May;

foreign—throughout the year (imported from Belgium, France, Holland).

Shopping and storage. Look for plump, well-bleached heads. If not needed for immediate use it will keep, well wrapped up, in the vegetable drawer of a refrigerator for ten days or in a cool larder for up to a week. If exposed to the light, chicory will turn green and develop a bitter flavour. It is sold by weight.

Cultivation. This is not difficult to grow. The fat folds of white leaves are obtained by excluding light. Sow in May and June in drills 1 cm deep in rows 40 cm apart. Thin seedlings to 30 cm apart. Remove flowery shoots during the summer to build up stray roots. During the summer the leaves can be cooked like spinach. In October twist off all the leaves to about 3 cm above the crown. The roots may then be lifted and packed tightly in boxes of sandy soil and covered with peat. Exclude all light. To force, store in a little warmth in a shed or cool greenhouse. Roots may be left in the ground and blanched by covering with an upturned flower-pot or a tent 30 cm high of black plastic to exclude all light. The blanched growth of young leaves is cut off close to the crown when 20 to 25 cm high.

CHINESE CABBAGE
Chinese cabbage has been available in Europe for only the past few years. This vegetable is known by a number of names including pte-tsai, wong-bok, shantung cabbage, chihli cabbage and Chinese leaves. Like other cabbages this variety from Eastern Asia has been cultivated since history began. It looks like a cross between a cos lettuce and a head of celery but is larger and heavier than both. Its base is long and white and it has whitish green, curly topped leaves. It has a crunchy texture and a more delicate flavour than cabbage.

Available: foreign—December to April (imported from Israel).

Shopping and storage. Look for firm heads and healthy leaves. Use as fresh as possible. See *Cabbage* for notes on storage.

Cultivation. Sow the seeds from mid-May for succession like lettuces. Sow outdoors in rich soil and keep thinned out, not transplanted.

CORN SALAD, see *Lamb's lettuce.*

COURGETTES, see *Marrow.*

CRESS, see *Mustard and cress.*

CUCUMBER
The plant is native to Asia. It has been cultivated in India for at least 3000 years and is said to have been introduced into England in 1573. The cucumber became very popular as a cooked vegetable. Eating it raw seems to be a modern idea. It went out of favour about a hundred years ago but interest revived in this century so that heavy imports are needed to supplement the home-grown varieties. Outdoor and glass-house cucumbers are grown in Essex, Hertfordshire and Kent. They have little food value but their main asset, the subtle and cooling quality of their flavour has been valued throughout history.

Available: home produced—throughout the year (not good in December); foreign—throughout the year (imported from the Canary Islands, France, Holland).

Shopping and storage. Most cucumbers on sale are about 30 cm long and 5 cm in diameter with a brilliant green shiny skin which is faintly ribbed. Top-grade cucumbers are straight, firm and evenly coloured with no sign of wilting. The eating quality of smaller curved cucumbers may be just as good and they will probably cost less. Many imported cucumbers are sold in transparent film which retains moisture and keeps them firm. This slows down but does not prevent deterioration. In late summer you may be able to purchase locally grown ridge cucumbers. These are an outdoor variety. They are usually smaller with a rougher, paler skin than hothouse specimens but are of equally good flavour and texture, and usually less expensive. Avoid soft, yellowish or spotty cucumbers. Use cucumbers promptly after purchase while still fresh and crisp. If you must store them, wrap them in paper, not plastic, as they need some circulation of air otherwise soft spots may quickly develop. Cover cut end of unused cucumber in kitchen foil or waxed paper held in place with an elastic band. A cucumber may also be put for a short time, stem first into a glass of cold water. Leftover ends of cucumber need not be wasted. They are excellent for rubbing over the skin to keep it soft and to soothe sunburn.

Cultivation: Greenhouse varieties should be sown in February to May in good seed compost in 100 mm peat pots. Plant out at four-leaf stage in a humus-rich compost in the greenhouse. Outdoor varieties may be started in the same way and planted out in May or can be sown in May directly into the ground outside. Water well in dry weather.

EGGPLANT, see *Aubergine.*

ENDIVE

Endive is a native of north eastern China. The date of its introduction to Britain is uncertain but it was well before 1548. Like many other vegetables it was out of fashion in Britain during the last century, though it remained popular in France. It has recently gained favour among gardeners, but is seldom seen in the shops. There are two main varieties, the curly staghorn endive and the broad-leaved Batavian endive. The curly staghorn looks like a green sponge with frizzy curly tendrils. It has a white centre where it has been bleached during cultivation. The Batavian endive, sometimes called the Batavian lettuce, looks like a rather coarse frilly lettuce. It has a heart similar to a cos lettuce. The heart is bleached by tying the outer leaves over it to exclude the light.

Available: home produced and foreign— September to May (imported from France).

Shopping and storage. Look for crisp, unblemished leaves. Use as soon as possible after purchase or harvesting as they do not store well.

Cultivation. Sow seeds thinly in drills 1 cm deep and 30 cm apart at intervals from April to August. Thin seedlings to 25 cm apart. They may need protection from winter frost. Blanch the leaves by excluding light with black plastic or upturned flower pots with holes covered, or by tying outer leaves over the hearts of Batavian varieties. Blanching takes about six weeks and improves the flavour. You can transplant the young plants to boxes and put them in a dark place. Harvest from August to March.

FENNEL

A fat, white root with a faintly aniseed flavour, it used to be grown mainly for the seeds which were used to flavour fish, bread and various medicines. The original plant has been developed in recent years and is now grown extensively on the continent as a vegetable crop. The root has thick, fleshy leaves arranged in two overlapping layers. These make an apple-shaped form about the size of a child's fist. It is hard and white, tinged with the palest green. The average bulb is about 7 cm in diameter weighing 100 to 150 g.

Available: foreign—October to March (imported from Italy and Southern France).

Shopping and storage. Choose roots which are really white with leaves lightly closed at the base. They are sold by the roots, charged by weight. Do not store the roots for more than a few days for new shoots will readily form at the base of the leaves.

Cultivation. Sow the seeds 2 cm deep in drills in light soil, in a sunny position in April. On no account let the developing bulbs dry out or they will become tough. When the bulbs begin to show, heap up the soil around them. The feathery foliage looks very delicate and pretty enough to be grown in a flower border.

KALE or KAIL

A form of non-hearted cabbage related to broccoli, turnips and radishes. The variety most often seen in greengrocers is the curly or Scotch kale; this is an attractive looking vegetable with dark blue-green leaves, crinkled and frilled at the edges. These grow from a thick central stem, near the top of which sprout tightly furled pale leaves. The flavour is similar to spinach. Allow 100 to 125 g per person, and prepare as for *Cabbage.*

Shopping. Kale should be fresh, firm and undamaged without decayed or yellow leaves.

Cultivation. Sow seed in April or May. Plant out in July 30 to 50 cm apart each way. Kale will stand up to very cold weather and is even improved by frost.

KOHL RABI

This is a hybrid of the cabbage family. The globular swollen stem is purple or white. The blue greens are similar to kale. The stem has a nutty taste, a blend of turnip and cabbage. It is popular on the continent though not so well known in this country and seldom seen in the shops.

Available: home produced—November to May.

Shopping. Choose firm, clean stems with fresh, crisp leaves.

Cultivation. Sow the seed in April and May in rows 35 cm apart. Thin out plants to 25 cm apart. The plants must be grown quickly to be fit to eat. Too slow growth causes woodiness of the stem. Harvest the roots when they are the size of tennis balls. They can be left in the ground until needed in mild areas, or stored like beetroots in colder areas for winter use.

LADIES FINGERS, see *Okra.*

LAMB'S LETTUCE

Sometimes known as corn salad, this is a European weed which has been improved by many years of cultivation. It is a very popular salad plant in France and Italy but less familiar in this country. The plant grows only 7 to 10 cm high in the form of a dark rosette-like bunch of leaves.

Available: home produced—during winter from October onwards.

Shopping and storage. Seldom available in greengrocers, the plant is very easily grown, Use as soon as possible after picking. Avoid prolonged storage.

Cultivation. Sow seeds in August and September for winter use and in the spring for summer and autumn. Sow in drills 25 cm apart. The plants do not need framing or blanching. A frame can be used to keep the plants in good condition throughout mid-winter. The plants should be eaten before they throw up flowery shoots in the spring as this spoils the flavour and texture. Pick the leaves while they are still small.

LEEKS

Leeks are among the oldest of cultivated vegetables. They have always been popular and until recently were taken for granted as an everyday, cheap vegetable. They were far more important than cabbages to our Saxon ancestors. Indeed the Saxon name for a vegetable garden was leek patch. Many English place names including Leighton Buzzard, Leckhampstead and Latton, are derived from leek-patch names. There is no authenticated reason why they should be associated with Wales and St David but there are many different legends supposedly explaining this. Leeks have returned to favour after years of being demoted to 'a poor man's' vegetable. They are no longer inexpensive.

Available: home produced—August to May; foreign—February to May (imported from Sweden, Norway, Denmark, Holland and Poland).

Shopping. Look for long, white, plump stems which are clean and unblemished and topped by fresh, dark green leaves. Refuse those with discoloured, yellowing or split leaves. They are sold in bundles or by weight.

Cultivation. Sow seeds in drills 30 cm apart in March and April. Thin plants out to 25 cm apart in July. You can ensure long white stems by transplanting the young plants in June into holes 15 to 20 cm deep. Make the holes with a dibber. Only the leaf tips should show above the rim. Do not fill in the hole with soil. Water plants thoroughly.

LETTUCE

Cultivated in Egypt and China from time immemorial, lettuce was known as a salad plant by the ancient Greeks and Romans. There are two main groups of lettuce, the cabbage and the cos. Cabbage lettuces have rather squat round heads, fairly solid hearts and an outer fringe of darker leaves. The cos lettuce has a prominent central rib. The heart tends to be less solid and the leaves crisper than the cabbage lettuce.

Available: home produced and foreign— throughout the year (imported from France, Holland, Israel, Italy, Jersey, Spain).

Shopping and storage. Look for well developed lettuces with fresh bright leaves. They should be free from discolouration and sliminess. If the outside leaves have been removed it is likely to be because the lettuce is stale. They should be eaten as soon as possible after harvesting. If kept for more than a day, they should be kept in a salad box in a refrigerator or wrapped in a cloth in a lidded pan or tin, in a cool place. If a lettuce is limp, leave it in ice cold water for a very short time before serving.

Cultivation. If you have cloches you can start lettuces off in February and March, otherwise wait until April. Sow seeds at fortnightly intervals in 1 cm deep drills 30 cm apart. Thin seedlings to 25 to 30 cm apart. Give them plenty of water so that they grow quickly without a check.

MARROW

A long round vegetable, the skin is usually green and may have white stripes or flecks. It is of the same family as melons, cucumbers, pumpkins and gourds. It was the Victorian gardener who decided that unripe marrows were unwholesome, and allowed them to reach immense proportions. Size became more important than flavour and texture resulting in the tasteless watery vegetable still served today. Fortunately the demand for small marrows is increasing so they are more readily available than in the past. There is no English name for small marrows so we have adopted the French and Italian names, courgettes and zucchini.

Two other kinds of summer marrow are occasionally available—custard marrow and Christophenes. The custard marrow, popular in America, looks like a pumped-up circle, white with scalloped edges. Christophenes, to be found in markets specializing in West Indian food, are more or less pear-shaped and covered with non-vicious prickles. They are rather lumpy with deep creases up the sides, light green or off-white in colour.

Available: home grown—July to November; foreign—all the year round (imported from France and Italy).

Shopping and storage. Choose young, firm, brightly coloured marrows not more than 30 cm long. Courgettes or zucchini should be not more than 20 cm long. Avoid bruised marrows as they deteriorate rapidly. Ripe marrows may be hung in nets suspended from the roof of a dry frost-proof room or shed. When stored in this way they should keep for three or four months.

Cultivation. Marrows are easily grown. It is worth doing this so that you can pick them while still small and so that you can use the flowers. Sow the seeds singly in 8 cm peat pots in April and plant out in a warm sunny position in rich soil in May or early June. Water well and make sure they never get dry. Cut the marrows when they are still small to ensure a regular and prolific crop.

MUSHROOMS

The cultivated mushrooms on sale in greengrocers and markets are perfectly safe to eat and are one of the best species. Until recently mushrooms tended to be regarded as a luxury but they have hardly risen in price for years and the cost remains almost the same throughout the year. They have been valued as food throughout the world since prehistoric times. Mushrooms exist in some 5000 varieties, most are edible and have been picked from the wild for centuries. They are universally popular, over 200 000 tonnes of commercially grown mushrooms being eaten throughout the world each year. Main growing areas in the United Kingdom are Kent, Surrey and Sussex followed by Lancashire and Yorkshire.

Available: home produced—throughout the year.

Shopping and storage. Sold at various stages of their growth in three main grades. Select the grade to suit the meal in mind. The grades are:
1 *Buttons.* Small unopened mushrooms with gills covered and veil intact. These have a mild flavour and delicate colour. Excellent for sauces, salads, garnishes and pickles.
2 *Cups.* The mushroom has started to open, the gills partly showing, the veil part broken. Recommended for slicing and frying or left whole for baking on their own or with a stuffing. Used to add flavour to pies, soups, stews, casseroles, etc.
3 *Open 'flats' with gills fully exposed.* These ripe mushrooms have the fullest flavour and are always the least expensive. Ideal for frying or grilling, sliced or whole.

Before buying check for freshness. Look at both the cup and the stalk. If the stalk is wrinkled the mushroom has been cut for some time. The cup of button mushrooms should be plump and white. The gills of open 'flats' should be dark but not black. Mushroom stalks can often be bought very cheaply. They are excellent for flavouring soups, stews, etc. Handle mushrooms gently. Avoid crushing them in the shopping basket. Mushrooms should be eaten as soon as possible after purchase. Really fresh mushrooms will keep for a few days in a refrigerator. Remove them from the bag or punnet and spread them on a flat dish. Cover and put in a refrigerator or really cool larder. If mushrooms become dried out because of evaporation during storage they can be revived by being immersed in boiling water for no more than one minute. They should then be carefully dried before being cooked.

Cultivation. Mushrooms can be grown at home but you must give them controlled conditions of fresh air, circulation, temperature and moisture to ensure success. Unless you are a very keen gardener this is one crop probably best left to the experts who can produce mushrooms at a much lower cost than the amateur.

MUSTARD AND CRESS

The punnets of mustard and cress to be purchased nowadays rarely include mustard and sometimes no cress. Rape seed is often used in place of mustard as it has a similar but milder flavour.

Available: home produced—all the year round.

Shopping and storage. Mustard and cress is sold still growing in punnets of peat. Avoid overlong mustard and cress as it is likely to lack flavour. Wilted leaves will not recover. Look for brightly coloured fresh leaves. Use on the day of purchase as it does not keep well. To prepare mustard and cress, clip with sharp scissors into a fine-meshed sieve, wash quickly in running water, then drain and remove tiny seeds.

Cultivation. This can be grown throughout the year though not outdoors during winter. Sow cress seeds three days before mustard in order to crop them on the same day. Grow them in the open ground in a fine tilth, in boxes of fine compost or peat, or indoors on pads of damp soft paper tissue. Traditionally young children grow them on pieces of damp flannel. Seeds need not be covered, just pressed into the surface of the peat or soil. Cover the seeds with paper until they germinate. Keep well watered.

OKRA

Also known as *Ladies' Fingers*. These green pods look like tiny gherkins pointed at one end with four or five sections filled with seeds. They are covered with a very fine down. When large, the pods are too fibrous to eat. Okra is a native of East Africa, prolific in South America, the Southern USA, West Africa and India. The rather glutinous texture is essential to the thick 'gumbo' dishes popular in Central America. It is used in curries and soups, in pickles, and as a vegetable.

Available: foreign—most of the year (imported from the Caribbean, West Africa).

Shopping. It can be purchased in areas where there is a large West Indian, Indian, or African community. Look for small unblemished green pods. Okra can be purchased tinned or dried.

Cultivation. Okra can be grown in mild areas or where a heated greenhouse is available. Sow the seeds in 5 cm peat pots in a temperature of 15°C in March and April. Keep moist but not wet. Plant out 45 to 50 cm apart when all danger of frost is over. Alternatively sow them where they are to crop 2 to 3 cm deep 45 cm apart in May.

ONIONS

Onions were already well known 5000 years ago and have been popular everywhere with the exception of India. Earliest historical records mention them. In ancient Egypt the onion was of major importance, used as an offering to the gods on altars and at funeral ceremonies. Records show that the labourers building the Pyramids had a diet with a preponderance of onions, leeks and garlic.

Onions have always been valued because they store well and provide an inexpensive flavouring for what would often have been a monotonous diet. The onion has also been regarded as an important medicinal plant, and it was thought to be a protection against a wide variety of illnesses.

There are several types of onion available in this country.
1 *Spanish type onions.* These are large, golden skinned, mild in flavour. Good for roasting, frying and eating raw.
2 *Tree or Egyptian onions.* Small, roundish, hard white onions with a strong flavour. Suitable for pickling.
3 *Shallots.* Small and pointed with a reddish skin. These have a delicate flavour and are excellent for cooking.
4 *Spring onions.* Smaller and longer in shape than ordinary onions, these have a white bulbous case and green leaves. Used raw for salads.
5 *Chives.* These have very tiny bulbs but it is not the bulbs but the green leaves which are clipped for flavouring. They are seldom obtainable in the shops but easily grown in the garden or in a flower pot on the kitchen window sill.

Onions grown in northern countries are on the whole pungent and juicy. Those from southern countries are milder, sweeter and better adapted for eating raw. Most British onions are grown in East Anglia.

Available: home produced—September to March; foreign—throughout the year imported from

Argentina, Canada, Chile, France, Egypt, Holland, Hungary, Israel, Poland, Portugal, South Africa, Spain, Italy, USA, Malta). Spring onions and chives are only available in the summer.

Shopping and storing. Look for firm, dry bulbs of a compact shape. Avoid discoloured or soft onions or those which are beginning to sprout. Thin-necked onions keep in good condition for longer than those with thick necks. Keep onions in a cool, dry place. They are good to use while they stay firm and do not sprout. Spring onions should be used as fresh as possible.

Cultivation. Sow seeds out of doors in March in rich, well-drained soil. Sow seeds 20 mm deep in drills 20 to 30 cm apart. Thin out young onions from 15 to 20 cm apart. Onion sets, small bulblets the size of acorns, can be planted out 15 to 20 cm apart in March and April. When the onions begin to mature in mid-August bend over the green tops just above the bulbs to hasten ripening. After a few weeks lift and dry carefully. Hang in ropes or bunches or lay out on slatted trays or wire mesh in any frost-free place. Spring onions should be sown in small successive batches from March to June and picked when ready for immediate use.

PARSLEY, HAMBURG TURNIP ROOTED
A hardy variety of parsley grown for its fleshy roots, eaten cooked or uncooked in the same way as carrots. The foliage can be used like ordinary parsley as a garnish or flavouring. The root is white and somewhat dry with a flavour rather like celeriac. It was considered a delicacy in England during the Victorian era. It is not often to be found in greengrocers' shops but is very easy to grow.

For availability, shopping, etc., see *Carrots* and *Parsnips.*

PARSNIPS
The parsnip, a relative of the carrot, is similar to it in shape but much larger with very pale brown skin and off-white flesh. Parsnips have never been widely cultivated, probably because they grew wild and were readily available when needed. They are still only eaten in any quantity in Britain and the USA. Cooks used little imagination in preparing dishes containing parsnips and the vegetable was

not seen to best advantage. Its reputation was not enhanced by its being a traditional lenten food to be served with salt cod. It is not often realized that it is a multipurpose vegetable. Apart from the root which is usually eaten, the stem is edible with a taste like celery and the deep green leaves excellent for winter salads. The unopened flowers of the plant used to be gathered and dried as a herb. Parsnips were often used as an ingredient for sweet dishes. It used to be thought that a new parsnip hung around the neck would keep off adders!

They are best not eaten until after the first frost which makes the roots mellow and golden. It is a valuable crop in that it can be left in the ground during the winter and can be dug up as needed.

Available: home grown—September to April.

Shopping. They can be purchased washed or unwashed; the latter tend to keep better. Avoid fanged or forked roots. Look for medium-sized parsnips, large ones are apt to have thick, tough cores. They should look fresh and be free of blemishes and soft, brown patches around the top. Parsnips, if dry, store well for up to two weeks.

Cultivation. Sow seed in drills in March 2 cm deep, 30 cm apart. Thin out to 15 cm between plants. Start harvesting in September. They can be left in the ground until needed.

PEAS
The pea is one of Britain's most popular vegetables. In this country about 74 000 hectares of peas are harvested each year, mainly in East Anglia. We eat 90 000 tonnes of frozen peas and 180 000 tonnes of tinned peas every year. Peas were the first vegetable to be canned and to be frozen commercially. They are used fresh or processed in practically every country in the world. They have a long history. They keep well when dried, and archaeologists have been able to prove their use in ancient times by discovery of remains. They were used in the Near East as far back as the eighth century BC. Herodotus, Horace and Pliny all recommend them as nourishing and inexpensive. It was much later that Italian gardeners of the late Renaissance developed better varieties of peas.

Peas are at their best gathered young and cooked immediately so it is advantageous to grow your own. A pea once podded has only 90 minutes before it starts to lose flavour. It is difficult to purchase good fresh peas because most of the pea production in this country is geared to the frozen, canned and dried food industry. Peas are bred which can stand the hazards of machine harvesting, give high yields and be suitable for commercial processing. This limits the varieties available in greengrocers' shops. Fresh baby peas are almost unobtainable in shops as they cannot be machine picked so are not profitable for the grower. However, although variety is limited, the quality and nutritive value of canned and frozen peas is consistently high. There is a large amount of wastage with podded peas, none with frozen or canned peas. Shelling is time consuming and the quality of the peas from greengrocers very variable. It is important to follow the instructions on the packet or can to gain the best flavour and food value from the peas. Once the can is opened, or frozen peas thawed, they deteriorate as quickly as podded peas.

There are innumerable varieties of peas available to the home grower. It is worth while studying seedsmen's catalogues to find out the up-to-date varieties available suitable for eating fresh and for home freezing. Marrowfat and wrinkled seeded varieties have a higher sugar content than round seeded peas. Different varieties sown in succession can give fresh young crops throughout late spring, summer and autumn. At the start of the season, when still very small, they can be eaten pods and all. In Britain we tend to call these baby peas *petit pois*, although this is the name of a special variety in France. Sugar peas (mange tout) have no parchment linings so the pod is edible.

Available: home produced—June to September.

Shopping. Avoid wet or overful pods as these will not be in prime condition. Dry wrinkled pods have been left on the plant too long so that, the sugar having been converted to starch, the flavour will be poor. Look for plump but not tight pods of a good colour and about 10 cm long. At its best a pea should disintegrate when pressed gently between thumb and finger. Purchase in small quantities for immediate use.

Cultivation. Sow early varieties during March and continue successive sowing until the end of June. Sow 30 cm deep 10 cm apart. Space the rows as wide apart as the variety is tall. Climbing varieties need support of sticks or netting. Dwarf varieties

need support from sticks or twigs. Supports help to increase yield and prevent slug damage and rotting.

PEPPERS
The shiny colourful pepper is the mildest flavoured but most decorative member of the capsicum family and is actually a non-poisonous nightshade. Most of the capsicum family have a hot taste and are dried and ground to produce spices such as cayenne, chilli and paprika. Sweet peppers are not very hot, but not without flavour. These attractive green, red and yellow vegetables were introduced to Europe by Columbus. The seeds he brought to Spain naturalized easily and spread quickly through the Mediterranean and central European countries. In different soils and climates they developed along different lines, aquired different names, and provided each country with the ingredient of a national recipe.

In Hungary and Austria they became the long pointed paprika, milder than chilli, but hotter than the sweet peppers we know. They are blanched and served whole and stuffed. In Spain, as pimentos, they have gradually become larger, rounder and milder to be used in pisto and ragout. In Mexico some of the peppers are so sweet that they are sold as sweets in some markets. In France they are used in ratatouille and piperade. Italians call them peperoni and add them to pasta dishes. The Greeks like them chopped raw in salads while in Eastern Europe they pickle them.

Green peppers are not yet ripe but some people prefer their flavour to the red ripe fruit. The yellow fruit is the most easily digested.

Available: imported all the year round except January from Israel, Italy and Spain.

Shopping and storage. Choose firm shiny fruits, light for their size. Use as soon as possible after purchase. If necessary store them in a refrigerator or cool place closely wrapped in foil or polythene. Peppers are the only vegetable not needing to be blanched before freezing.

Cultivation. Sow seeds in March or April in a temperature of 18°C. Prick out seedlings into 6 cm peat pots. In early June they can be planted out in a greenhouse border, or outside, or repotted to grow on a sunny window sill.

PLANTAIN

This is really a tropical fruit related to the banana but because it must be cooked to be palatable it is usually treated as a vegetable. Plantains look like large bananas about 25 to 30 cm long but they are coarser textured and are not sweet even when ripe. They must be cooked to avoid a starchy raw flavour. They become bitter if overcooked due to a tannin component. They can be boiled in salted water, or fried, or combined with meat, cheese or eggs to make a variety of dishes.

The plantain was brought to southern Europe via Africa by Arab traders from India. A Spanish missionary priest went to the West Indies in 1516 taking with him plantain shoots which he thought might be grown successfully in the tropics. They lived up to his expectation and flourished. However, we know now that this was only to be expected as, unknown to him, plantains were already growing at that time in many areas of Central America.

Plantains are usually available from West Indian shops and market stalls. They are sold in all degrees of ripeness from green through yellow to brown. Recipes usually indicate the degree of ripeness needed.

Available: foreign—most of the year (imported from the West Indies).

POTATOES

This is yet another New World vegetable, cultivated by the Incas of Peru as far back as 800 BC. Potatoes were held in high esteem, worthy of important religious rituals at planting and harvest time.

The first Europeans to realize the value of the crops were Spanish soldiers. This discovery proved of greater value to later generations than any other treasures they might have found. The Incas had already made selective cultivation of many varieties including those suitable for cold mountainous regions. Their method of drying potatoes for storage was basically the same as that used today for the 'newly invented' dried potato.

It is believed that the first potatoes in Europe were those brought by a monk returning home to Spain. Cultivation quickly spread through Italy, Austria and Switzerland. It is not certain who first brought potatoes to Britain. Sir Francis Drake, Sir John Hawkins, and Sir Walter Raleigh have each been given the credit for this. All we know for

certain is that by 1700 it had become the basic food of the poor in Ireland, while in England it was merely grown as a novelty. It was later accepted by the people of the north of England but for some time there was prejudice against it in the south. It was only after a prolonged series of bad harvests after 1750 that farmers acknowledged the value of the crop. Even then this was only as winter feed for cattle. It was the advent of the Napoleonic wars and the possibility of famine that really brought potatoes into popularity.

In Ireland the peasants had become almost entirely dependent on potatoes for food, using any other crops they grew to pay rent. This dependence proved fatal for many. Failure of the crop due to potato blight in 1845 and 1846 caused widespread starvation and death from a typhus epidemic. Many survivors emigrated to America. Starvation and emigration halved the population within a few years. Ireland is only now recovering from this calamity.

We are no longer dependent on just a few basic foods for survival but we would certainly miss the potato if it were no longer available. Plant breeders are constantly searching for new varieties. There are at least 2000 types known to experts. Only a few dozen of these are grown commercially and not all of these are generally available to the public. Potatoes are available throughout the year from the early potatoes which are dug from May onwards to the main crops which are lifted from September for use throughout the winter.

A potato is the swollen end of an underground stem. It is a stem tuber not a true root like a carrot. The tuber serves the potato plant as a source of food, the new shoots growing from the 'eyes'. Different soils and climates produce potatoes of different texture and taste each particularly suitable for certain methods of cooking. The seed potatoes used throughout the British Isles are grown mainly in Scotland. Here the climate and other geographical conditions ensure that the seed potatoes will be free from infection by virus diseases. Over 280 000 hectares of potatoes are planted in Great Britain alone and over six million tonnes are harvested. In addition to this new potatoes are imported from overseas.

The potato has proved very adaptable to the needs of modern life. There is a thriving industry

POTATO CHART

Key
(1) excellent; (2) very good; (3) good; (4) can be used for this purpose, but should only be jacket baked or chipped late in the season (August to September).

		BOILED	MASHED	JACKET BAKED	ROAST WITH MEAT	CHIPPED	SALAD USE
Early potatoes (late May to end of August)							
Arran Pilot	Creamy white flesh. Soft but not mealy in cooking. Mild flavour.	2			3	3	2
Red Craig Royal	Pale cream flesh. Close texture. Rarely discolours after cooking.	2		4	3	3	2
Home Guard	Creamy white flesh. Close texture. Rarely discolours after cooking. Delicate flavour.	2			3	3	2
Maris Peer	Pale cream flesh. Firm. Rarely discolours after cooking.	2		4	2	2	2
Ulster Prince	White flesh. Waxy texture becoming floury on maturity. Rarely discolours after cooking.	2			3	4	3
Maincrop (from September onwards)							
Desiree	Pale cream flesh. Very rarely discolours after cooking. Mealy texture.	2	2	2	2	2	4
Golden Wonder	Cream flesh. Mealy texture. Mild flavour. Excellent keeping quality. Only generally available in Scotland.	2	2	1	2	3	
Redskin	Pale lemon flesh of mealy texture. Popular in the North and Scotland.	3	2	3	3	1	
Kerrs Pink	Creamy white flesh. Some surface sloughing on boiling. A floury potato. Usually available in Scotland only.	2	2	2	2	2	
King Edward	Creamy white flesh of mealy texture. Very rarely discolours on cooking. Very good quality potato.	1	1	1	1	2	4
Majestic	Creamy white. Mealy texture. Slight tendency to discolour. Good keeping quality.	3	3	2	2	2	4
Maris Piper	Creamy white flesh. Mealy texture. Very rarely discolours on cooking.	2	2	3	2	3	
Pentland Crown	Creamy white flesh of close texture.	3	3	2	3	3	4
Pentland Dell	Creamy white. Close texture.	3	3	2	3	3	4
Pentland Ivory	White flesh. Mealy texture.	2	2	2	3	3	

converting potatoes to convenience foods such as instant potato powder, flakes, granules and chip powders, potato crisps and sticks, canned potatoes and frozen chipped potatoes. The traditional British meal of fish and chips is responsible for the consumption of ever increasing quantities of potatoes each year.

Potato production is linked with the fishing industry because whenever there is a shortage of potatoes the consumption of fish rapidly declines.

Contrary to popular belief the potato, taken in moderation, is not a fattening food. An average sized potato contains no more calories than half a grapefruit or a small banana. It is the additional ingredients used when cooking and serving potatoes, such as butter, cream and cheese, which are the culprits not the potato itself. A regular intake of sensible quantities of potatoes can provide an important source of Vitamin C and iron. New potatoes are particularly rich in Vitamin C (ascorbic acid).

When preparing potatoes for babies or people with weak digestions it is sensible to avoid new potatoes altogether, and from old potatoes to choose the mealy textured type of potato rather than the waxy varieties.

The table shows the fifteen most popular varieties grown in this country. Usage rating is shown thus: (1) excellent; (2) very good; (3) good; (4) can be used for this purpose, but should only be jacket baked or chipped late in the season (August to September).

It is unfortunate that most potatoes are rarely offered on sale by name to the general public. However, if enough people persistently asked for potatoes by name retailers might think it worth while to label them and to provide more variety than just nameless 'Reds' or 'Whites'.

Available: home produced—throughout the year; foreign—mainly early potatoes (imported from Belgium, Canary Islands, Cyprus, France, Holland, Israel, Italy, Jersey, Malta, Morocco, Spain).

Shopping and storage. Choose firm, well-shaped potatoes free from blemishes and decay and without excessive clinging soil. They may be purchased washed but will not store as well as unwashed potatoes. Avoid green or sprouting potatoes. All potatoes contain a poison called solanine and probably other toxicants as well. Normally the quantity is much too small to matter, merely giving the potato its characteristic taste. However occasionally it reaches dangerous levels in tubers that have turned green and in potato sprouts. In most cases peeling away the green flesh will solve the problem. People with digestive problems and expectant mothers should take especial care not to eat green potatoes. If you use a large quantity of *main crop potatoes* and can store them during the winter it is economical to buy in bulk. You can get large packs in some shops or direct from the grower, either delivered from the shop or collected by yourself. Check over the potatoes. Take out any that are damaged and use these first. Store potatoes in a cool, dry place such as a larder, cellar or frost-free shed. They should be kept in the dark, even just in a thick brown paper bag or a sack. Light causes greening and a bitter taste. Store away from strong smelling foods or things such as paraffin. Purchase *early potatoes* frequently in small quantities. The sooner they are eaten after being dug up the better they taste. The skin should be moist rather than dry. It should rub off easily. Handle them gently as they bruise easily.

Cultivation. Potatoes are planted in March and April. If planted earlier they run the risk of being destroyed by frost. Potatoes should be ready for digging from July to October depending on the variety. Plant seed potatoes 15 to 20 cm apart in furrows 30 cm apart. They should be covered in 5 to 8 cm of soil. Young plants should be earthed up regularly to ensure that the developing tubers are well covered with sufficient soil to prevent light reaching them.

PUMPKIN

Pumpkins have been cultivated since ancient times in Europe, the Middle East and the Americas but the name, derived from the Greek for melon, means 'cooked by the sun' and goes back only to the seventeenth century. They are from the same family as marrows, melons and cucumbers. They were very popular in this country from the sixteenth century until recent times when they went out of fashion. There are many old recipes making use of this vegetable. They are again to be seen for sale in greengrocers in the autumn. Colours go from greenish white to green, and yellow to the strongest shades of orange. Shapes are as varied as the colours. They can grow to an enormous size; one variety called Hundredweight grows to match its name. Most of those available in the shops are about the size of netballs. They are traditionally used to make Hallowe'en lanterns, the scooped out flesh being used to make soups and sweets or served as a vegetable.

For details about shopping, etc., see *Marrow*.

RADISHES
This is such a long established plant that its origins are obscured in antiquity. The present-day radish is smaller than those grown in the past when they were used as a main vegetable and a valuable source of radish-seed oil rather than just a garnish or salad plant. There are white and black radishes as well as the familiar scarlet roots. They may be globular or elongated.

Available: home produced—April to September; foreign—December to May (imported from Holland, France and Italy).

Shopping. Sold in bunches. The size of the bunches varies with the season, being smaller early in the year. Look for young, crisp, fresh roots. Avoid split or badly shaped roots and wilted foliage. They do not store well but will recover some crispness in ice cold water.

Cultivation. Very easy to grow. Sow seeds thinly about 5 cm deep from March onwards at three-weekly intervals.

SALSIFY
Long black or white roots with white flesh and a flavour not unlike that of oysters, hence its alternative name of vegetable oyster. The black variety known as *Scorfonera* has the better flavour. Salsify is not very well known in the British Isles, but it is popular on the continent. Although grown primarily for the roots, the young leaves in spring may be eaten in salads. The plant has tall, pinkish purple flowers and is handsome enough to grow in the flower border. In Spain it was grown as a remedy for snakebite

Available: home grown—December to March.

Shopping and storage. Avoid pencil-thin roots as they are too thin to scrape or peel. The roots do not keep well so purchase for immediate use only.

Cultivation. Sow seeds 2 cm deep in drills 25 cm apart in April. Thin seedlings to 25 cm apart. Lift roots in the autumn and store in a damp or cool shed for immediate use or leave in the ground until needed.

SPINACH
The origins of this plant are vague. It appears to be indigenous to the Persian area, not appearing in Europe until the twelfth century. The earliest written record is a Chinese one stating it to be introduced to Nepal in 647 AD.

Poor cooking plus the constant preaching to children that 'it's good for you' have combined to make most people wary of spinach. This is a pity because the damp climate of the British Isles helps to give us some of the most succulent spinach in the world. Properly cooked it is a most useful vegetable. It goes well with cheese, bacon, eggs, meat, mushrooms and onions. It can be used for soups, flans, pasta and soufflés.

There are two types of true spinach, summer or round seeded and winter prickly seeded. In addition there are two similar leaves, spinach beet and New Zealand spinach both sold under the name of 'chards'. Spinach beet or perpetual spinach lasts well into the winter and does not go to seed as quickly as true spinach. New Zealand spinach is rather drier and tougher than the others.

Available: home produced—all the year round with most in March and April.

Shopping and storage. Look for fresh green leaves free from yellowing, flowering shoots and hard stalks. The summer spinach is light green while winter spinach is darker and slightly tougher. Spinach does not store well. It wilts quickly and turns yellow so purchase just enough for immediate use.

Cultivation. Sow seeds in drills 2 cm deep, 30 cm wide and thin out to 30 cm apart. Sow summer spinach successively every three weeks from February to April. Sow winter spinach from August to mid-September.

SWEDES
Swedes are members of the cabbage family. The roots are large and round in shape with pinkish skin and yellow or white flesh. A seventeenth-century development of the turnip, they are known also as swedish turnips or turnip-rooted cabbage. They are grown mainly in Devon and Somerset.

They can be used on their own, mixed with other root vegetables or added to soups and casseroles.

Available: home produced—September to May.

Shopping. Look for firm, unblemished roots. The small young roots, about the size of a table tennis ball, have a better flavour than fully grown specimens.

Cultivation. Sow seeds between March and August in light rich soil 1 cm deep and in rows 35 cm apart. Thin out to 15 to 25 cm apart.

SWEETCORN

Maize probably originated in either the Andean regions of South America or in Mexico and was being cultivated there between 7000 to 5000 BC. It is possibly the oldest of all cultivated plants. The primitive maize cob was a mere twenty or thirty millimetres long but its size bears no relation to the importance of the crop in the days of the great Indian cultures. Maize was not only a staple food but valued as currency, building material and jewellery. It provided a variety of drink, was used as a ritual offering to the gods and was the subject of many legends. It was taken to Spain and Africa in the early sixteenth century and from there its 'dispersal' was rapid. There is mention of it in Chinese writing as a court tribute in 1550.

Selection and breeding of the descendants of these early coarse grasses has evolved different classes of maize including those used for cattle feed, flour, popcorn and corn on the cob or sweetcorn.

Maize is still an important commodity apart from its value as a basic food. The stalks are used for a variety of materials from building boards and upholstery fillings to explosives. The cobs are used in the manufacture of synthetic fibres and rubber, plastics, paint and soap. Cornmeal flour, cornflour, cornstarch, corn oil and numerous breakfast cereals are made from maize. In addition it is used commercially in the making of soluble coffee, soup powder, ice cream, sausages, jam and table jellies. It would be difficult to find another staple food which has had a greater influence on our lives.

However, though it was known to the prehistoric Indian farmer it was not until this century that sweetcorn became really popular. Until recently we have had to import all the maize we use but in the last few years it has been grown successfully as a field crop in the southern counties of Britain.

Available: home grown and foreign—July to September (imported from Canada and USA).

Shopping and storage. Corn on the cob is eaten when still immature; later the sweet kernel turns to starch. Choose ears with fresh green leaves. The golden stalks should be just tinged with brown. The kernels should be well developed right to the top of the ear but not jammed tightly together. Pull back the silk and press the kernel with a finger nail. If hard it is too old, if watery it is too young. It should be tender and milky. Maize should be kept cool and moist from the time of harvesting. If possible put it in a refrigerator as soon as you get home and use it as soon as possible.

To eat corn. There are special cob holders, otherwise hold the cob in the fingers eating as tidily as possible, spreading with butter as required.

Cultivation. Seeds can be sown individually in 10 cm peat pots under glass in April and planted outside 25 to 30 cm apart in rows 60 cm apart. You must plant at least four rows to ensure pollination. It can be sown directly into the soil, 2 cm deep in mid-May.

SWEET POTATOES

Sweet potatoes were cultivated by the Indians of Peru at least three thousand years ago. They are now the staple vegetable in South America, the West Indies and throughout the Pacific area, and naturalized in all warm countries.

They look like rather large, oddly-shaped potatoes. There are several varieties with skin colour ranging from nearly white to brown, and from pink to purple. The sweet moist flesh may be white, yellow, orange or purple. It is the white variety that you will be most likely to find in this country in shops and markets where there is a West Indian community.

Columbus was the first European to eat sweet potatoes. He likened them to large radishes. The vegetable was brought to Spain soon after and introduced to Britain in the sixteenth century. They were accepted because of the sweet taste similar to the already familiar parsnip. The ordinary potato, which came later and gradually replaced them in common usage, did not receive the same enthusiastic reception. Although they are both called potatoes they are not related in any way. Sweet potatoes are the tuberous roots of a tropical vine related to the Morning Glory. They are not yams, the name often given to them erroneously in American cookery books.

Available: Imported throughout the year from the West Indies and South America.

Shopping. Look for sweet potatoes with unscratched skins.

TOMATO

This is another plant which has its origins in the Peruvian Andes. The first wild tropical tomatoes had little flavour. They were very small, soft and yellow with tissue-thin skins. The Incas finding them to be edible made use of this indigenous food along with a plant of the same family, the wild potato. Their cultivation spread to Equador and Bolivia and on to Central America following the Spanish invasion. The Aztecs of Mexico also cultivated them. Spaniards returning home in 1583 brought the golden fruit to Europe calling them by their Spanish Mexican name *tomata.* They flourished and soon became popular in Spain and Italy. They were introduced into England in 1596. Few people risked eating them. The bright colouring was thought to be Nature's warning against the danger of poison. They were grown in gardens as decorative plants, the over-ripe fruit being used as missiles to be thrown at unfortunates in the pillory or at actors who failed to meet the required standard! It was not until 1818 that the London Horticultural Society gave the tomato recognition as having value as a food. Even then it was still not regarded as quite respectable to eat tomatoes. People still needed reassurance that it would not cause gout or cancer.

Over 90 000 tonnes of tomatoes are now grown in Britain alone. This is supplemented by imports from Holland, Spain and the Canary Islands enabling us to eat tomatoes all the year round. Tomato growers have to comply with EEC standards of grading quality. They are also graded by size—A being the largest and going down to F. Quality in grading terms means smooth skinned, round tomatoes free from blemishes and disease. No one can judge flavour from appearance but this is at its best when the tomatoes are just picked.

Available: home grown—March to November; foreign—throughout the year (imported from Canary Islands, Holland, Spain).

Shopping. Look for fruit of a good shape, round or oval, and of good even colour. They should be matt rather than glossy. Avoid damaged fruit. Green tomatoes are sometimes sold cheaply in markets. These can be ripened at home or used for chutney. Buy tomatoes frequently in small quantities. They are less expensive in the summer.

Cultivation. Sow seeds in good compost in January and February for early greenhouse crops, and March for summer and autumn and for outdoor planting. Prick out when large enough to handle into peat pots so that, at planting time, they are strong and sturdy with first fruit sets. Spray the flower trusses to improve fruit sets. Many people prefer to purchase young seedlings. There are several new varieties of tomatoes which can be grown all the year round even in window boxes or pots on window sills.

TURNIPS

The turnip is similar in shape to the swede but the skin is white and pale green and the inside flesh is white. The most important areas for turnip production in this country are the Home Counties, Hampshire, Worcestershire and Cheshire.

The cultivation of turnips is older than recorded history. Because of its excellent storage qualities it was a very good standby as a winter food for both animals and men. It was already being cultivated in India before the Aryan invasion of about 1500 BC. Early Greek and Roman writers show that the turnip was much valued. There were food snobs even then and it was regarded as more suitable for country people and the poor rather than well-to-do town dwellers. In Britain, they were liked by the Romans and Saxons. In the time of Elizabeth I, Flemish refugees introduced improved strains of the vegetable.

Available: Home grown—October to March.

Shopping. Look for firm, unblemished roots. Avoid any with wormholes or spongy and soft brown patches. Like swedes they are at their best while still small, preferably the size of a table tennis ball. Early turnips may be cylindrical or globular. The globular roots are sweeter and have a better flavour. Buy early roots little and often. Turnips may be purchased washed or unwashed.

Cultivation. Turnips grow quickly. Seeds sown in

April can produce tennis-ball sized turnips a month later. For winter use sow seeds 2 cm deep during May and June in drills 45 cm apart. Thin out roots to 30 cm apart.

WATERCRESS

Thought to be of Persian origin, watercress has grown wild in Britain and been gathered as a medicinal herb as well as for food for over 2000 years. The Romans thought it helped them to make bold decisions and was of use in treating mental illness, while the young ladies of the seventeenth century ate quantities of it to help clear freckles which were then unfashionable.

In the past, when great areas of the country were sparsely populated, it was fairly safe to gather wild watercress from the sides of streams and rivers. It would not be sensible to do so today. Watercress still grows wild but there is now a danger from sewage pollution and also from the liver fluke which attacks human beings as well as sheep. Do not purchase watercress which is not marked with the producer's name. The National Farmers Union runs a scheme of accreditation for the hundred or more professional growers. This more or less guarantees that the cress leaves the farm free from contamination. Watercress is the only vegetable which is never imported.

The main growing areas in this country are in Hampshire but cress farms can be found as far north as Lincolnshire and south as far as Dorset. It is a highly specialized industry.

To grow watercress successfully you need plenty of clean water, between one and two and a half million litres a hectare every day. A machine has recently been invented which should be able to do some of the work automatically. This should help keep down production costs. Watercress is good value for money. It has not increased in price for over thirty years.

Available: home produced—throughout the year.

Shopping and storage. Look for the producer's mark. It is sold by the bunch. At its best it is long, fresh and a good colour. It may be light or dark green according to the variety. Rinse quickly in cold water and remove any odd roots and yellow leaves. Do not soak. If the watercress cannot be used immediately it must be kept in a cool place away from strong light. If you have no refrigerator, trim stems and place loosely in a jar of cold water. If you have a refrigerator, shake off surplus water and put into a polythene box or bag. Seal and put into salad drawer away from the icebox. Do not trim the stems too short as these are as nutritious as the leaves.

YAMS

Different species of yam have been cultivated and grown wild in Africa, South East Asia, and Eastern South America for centuries. The edible root of a climbing plant it looks like a really huge, rough skinned, badly shaped potato. A starch product called guiana arrowroot is extracted from yams for use in cookery and confectionery. It is sometimes confused with sweet potatoes because these are often called yams in some parts of the United States. These are quite different vegetables, though yams may be cooked in the same ways as sweet potatoes. Yams are usually available in areas where there is an African or West Indian population.

Available: foreign—throughout the year (imported from West Africa and the West Indies).

ZUCCHINI, see *Marrow.*